The Bitter Pill

The Bitter Pill

An Insider's Shocking Exposé of the

Irish Health System

Doctor X

HODDER
HEADLINE
IRELAND

*The author and publishers would like to express their sincere
thanks to Susie Long for her kind permission to reproduce
the transcript of her letter to RTÉ's 'Liveline' (Jan 07).*

A CIP catalogue record for this title is available from the
British Library.

ISBN 978 0 340 95132 3

Typeset in Sabon by Hodder Headline Ireland
Cover design by Anú Design

Printed and bound in Great Britain by Clay's Ltd, St Ives plc
Hodder Headline Ireland's policy is to use papers that are
natural, renewable and recyclable products and made from
wood grown in sustainable forests. The logging and
manufacturing processes are expected to conform to the
environmental regulations of the country of origin.

Hodder Headline Ireland
8 Castlecourt Centre
Castleknock
Dublin 15, Ireland
A division of Hachette Livre, 338 Euston Road, London
NW1 3BH, England

Contents

This book is dedicated to the Irish Intern: a group of young men and women who work endlessly, tirelessly and who do their best to discharge their duties to the highest standards of medical practice and ethics despite the broken system around them.

MEDICAL HIERARCHY FOR HOSPITAL DOCTORS
Consultant
Specialist Registrar (consultant-in-training)
Registrar
Senior House Officer (SHO)
Intern
(The last two positions are held by the junior doctor)

'For the past few years I have had access to the health services from the inside. It is this insider's perspective that is so often lacking in the media-driven analysis of the problems plaguing the health system. The horrific stories we read every day in the newspapers and hear on the radio – people left on trolleys in A&E; gross mismanagement of patients in ludicrous circumstances; a young mother turned away from hospital, only to be discovered later, drowned in the river with her two young children – these stories, while undeniably inexcusable, are not actually the problems, but rather the symptoms. They are the horrifying results of a deeper, pervasive and systemic disease that has colonised the Irish health system and threatens to disable it entirely.'

The Reasons Why

In autumn 2006 I was sitting in the back of a taxi, which was driving me to the Irish Medical Council, where I would renew my registration. Under time pressure and with a hundred and one things playing on my mind, I was surprised when the taxi-driver put a question to me:

So, Doctor, what do you think is the problem with the Irish health system? Why is it that, despite being one of the richest countries in Europe and the world, our health services rival those of Third World countries in many respects?

My first reaction was 'How should I know?' After all, I'm only a grunt, a lowly non-consultant hospital doctor doing his best to not mess up and to juggle a busy work and social schedule.

Nonetheless, the question gave me pause to think. More than that, as the weeks passed the relevance of the taxi-driver's questions began to play enormously on my mind and, perhaps for the first time since I had begun to study medicine almost a decade earlier, I started to give serious consideration to my ability to answer it.

I began to realise that although I may be only a lowly paid junior doctor, I do in fact have a unique viewpoint on the situation. After all, I've been to medical school and trained in Ireland. I have seen and experienced at first-hand at least ten different hospitals and interacted with hundreds, if not thousands, of health professionals in all branches of the service. I have had to fight against the problems that arise from day to day, again and again, over and over. In fact, as a non-consultant hospital doctor, I am the first line of defence in the system. If everyone else refuses to do a job, it will undoubtedly fall to me. I know the system in a way other commentators cannot: I know it as an employee who has struggled to do his job in the face of myriad obstacles. In order to understand why I chose to write this book, you need to understand where I am coming from – and that means you need to understand just what a day in the life of a junior doctor in an Irish hospital is like.

Junior doctors are involved in almost every

aspect of patient care and management, from issues of daily patient needs to overall patient management and the successful running of the medical team. When a patient comes through the door in the A&E department of any hospital, it is the junior doctor he/she will encounter first. We are the care staff who talk to them, take note of the symptoms that have brought them to hospital, as well as their past medical history and any other information that might be pertinent to their admission and care. We then perform a thorough physical examination of all of their systems to further elucidate the problem and ensure no other illness is missed. We make an assessment based on this information and formulate an initial treatment plan. This may be as simple as starting someone on an antibiotic or an intravenous drip or performing blood tests, or more complicated, such as preparing them for emergency surgery. If I am unsure as to the optimum treatment for the patient, I consult with my peers. We pool our knowledge and resources to solve the problem. If we are still unsatisfied, we can ask more senior non-consultant doctors about the best course of action.

The consultants are the last port of call and are very rarely involved during the initial process. The registrar on call will disturb them only if absolutely necessary. When a patient comes into the hospital in the middle of the night in an emergency situation – perhaps their heart has stopped, or they are unable to breathe – the junior doctors are involved in their immediate treatment and resuscitation. In Irish hospitals it is unusual for consultants to be present at night-time, therefore it falls to the non-consultant hospital doctors to stabilise the patient.

It is the junior doctor in A&E who makes a decision whether to admit a patient to hospital or to recommend home treatment with out-patient follow-up. In some hospitals, prior to making a decision to admit a person, junior doctors are required to consult a senior colleague in charge of the department at the time (not necessarily a consultant). In other hospitals, it is left entirely to the junior doctor's own discretion.

Either way, once the decision to admit has been made, the patient is referred to the on-call junior doctor, usually a S.H.O. (Senior House Officer – though the word 'senior' here is misleading), depending on whether the problem is medical or surgical in nature. In some of the bigger hospitals, this is further subdivided into various specialities. The junior doctor on call then does his/her own assessment of the patient and formally admits the patient to the hospital. He/she performs or organises the basic set of investigations which are routine for most patients admitted to hospital, such as blood tests, urine analysis and x-rays. In addition to this, the junior doctor will also arrange for any other investigations he/she feels are necessary for the case in hand.

Once all this has been set in motion, the junior doctor initiates the beginning of the long-term management plan that will ultimately lead to recovery and discharge. This includes prescription of any medications required. The patient is then reviewed regularly, as necessary. During this time the junior doctor must also keep an eye on the various investigations he/she has ordered, in order to quickly interpret the results as they come in and vary the management plan accordingly.

In the morning, when the consultant on-call the previous day arrives in, there is a post-call ward round with the full medical team. The junior doctor 'presents' the patient to the consultant and the team, giving them a detailed medical history, the results of all the investigations completed thus far, a description of treatment to that point and an explanation of the management plan. It is based on this information, which has been collected and collated by the junior doctor and presented in a succinct and precise manner, along with his own assessment, that the consultant then makes the decisions regarding the further management of that patient.

This process is repeated for every patient admitted under that medical team.

On the ward, the junior doctors set about implementing this treatment plan. If a patient needs a blood test, more often than not it will be the junior doctor who takes the sample, sends it off, then checks up on the results. If an x-ray or other scan needs to be organised, the junior doctor fills in the request forms and presents them to the relevant department. Sometimes he/she will have to talk to the radiology consultant and explain the history of the patient and the level of urgency of the scan. In the event that the facilities needed to perform the scan are unavailable in the hospital, which happens often in the case of MRI or other specialised scans, the junior doctor has to telephone various hospitals and speak to the radiologists there to request that they scan the patient. As well as organising for the scan to be done, the junior doctor must also make arrangements for the administrative department to pay for it and ensure that the patient leaves at the right time, with the right level of support. Once the scan has been done, the junior doctor has to chase up these results and inform the consultant when they become available so that the management plan can be adapted.

The junior doctor must also keep the medical notes of the patients up-to-date. At least once a day the current condition of the patient must be documented, including any improvements or worsening of their symptoms, the latest results of various tests and the revised treatment plan for each patient. This information is vital not only for current management but also for any future admissions. In the unhappy circumstance that problems arise later, the information collected during the patient's stay in hospital can be helpful in evaluating what went wrong and why. Many consultants prefer not to make notes in the patients' charts, or to limit such comments to the minimum level possible. As a result, the junior doctor often documents the assessment and recommendations given by the consultant during the ward round. If you look at any medical chart hanging from the end of a patient's bed, there will be a signature at the bottom of each entry indicating the source: most are junior doctors.

Keeping track of all assigned patients is also the work of the junior doctor, who must maintain a list of which patients are on his/her team and where those patients are located around the hospital. It is common for one of the junior doctors to lead the ward round, taking the rest of the medical team to visit all the patients in the most efficient manner possible. If the consultant doesn't have time that day to see all the patients, the junior doctors perform a 'dry round', whereby the list of patients is gone through quickly with the consultant, who is updated with all relevant information. If you ever need intravenous medication, it is the junior doctor who will put the cannula in your arm and give you the first dose of the medication. He/she will make sure you are not allergic to any of the medications you are being given and will remain on hand in case of any unpredicted adverse reaction. If a patient develops new symptoms or if current ones worsen, or if they have any questions about their treatment, it is the junior doctor who is called to the bedside to talk through their problems and options. The junior doctor will also liaise with GPs, keeping them updated as to the progress of the patient. He/she writes letters informing the patient's GP of the cause of admission, the treatment given and the follow-up required to ensure the patient's care is not abandoned post-discharge.

Junior doctors also keep in regular contact with the families of patients. While on occasion the family does get to speak to the consultant, in the majority of cases it is the junior doctor who is called to address their concerns and keep them informed. In this way, the junior doctor also acts as a go-between, passing on the family's worries to the consultant and the rest of the medical team. This is a role that nurses engage in, too, and they are excellent at it. However, when the question is related to the direct medical management of the patient and future treatment, a doctor is usually required to provide that information.

Sometimes, the most valuable services the junior doctor provides are the intangible ones: offering a sympathetic ear, or simply sitting down and talking to patients about their illness and the effect it is having on them and their family. I believe this is probably the most important task of all, but, sadly, due to the hectic nature of our jobs, it is the one that we most often have to forgo – usually more to the detriment of our souls than the well-being of our patients. Thankfully, junior doctors are supported by many courageous and dedicated nurses, who pick up the slack in this regard.

Last, but not least, when the in-patient treatment is complete and the patient is ready for discharge, it is the junior doctor who must ensure that they are prescribed with all the medication needed and that they have appropriate follow-up. If a sick note is required for work or a social services certificate, it's our job to provide this.

As a junior doctor, I participate in all of these roles to varying degrees, as required. I am actively involved in all aspects of patient management and must deal daily with every little problem that arises, be it medical, managerial or bureaucratic. Of course,

I can, and do, refer to my senior colleagues and consultants for advice, but I am still, like all junior doctors, expected to keep the whole machine running smoothly, even as the malfunction alarm rings deafeningly.

As I have said, the horrific stories we hear regularly, of how the health system is failing patients, are not the problems, but the symptoms. It is the cumulative effect of these 'symptoms' that manifests istelf daily before our eyes. And it is only by recognising and addressing these fundamental problems that we can begin to make any progress towards a more efficient, more caring and more equal health system. It is already painfully obvious to the Irish taxpayer that simply hurling money in the general direction of the HSE in a haphazard fashion fails to produce any tangible results. Obviously, many people involved in the health services are aware of these issues on various levels. I have no doubt that top-ranking politicians and government ministers are also well-informed. Change is a scarce commodity, however. Time and time again we are subjected to half-hearted, 'band-aid' solutions that are sundered apart at the first step. The bottom line is that, up until now, there have been too many vested interests and personal agendas; too much politics, power-play and petty bullying.

So, how do we set about addressing and, more importantly, solving these problems? While no consensus has been reached to answer this question, it is clear to all concerned that we need a radical rethink, on many levels. The truth is, a long and difficult process lies ahead of us if we are to effect any real change within the Irish healthcare system. But first things first: we need to name and admit to the issues that are preventing improvement and progress. This, I hope, will be my contribution.

I have both a personal motive and an idealistic motive in writing this book. First, the personal. When the idea for this book first began to take shape, I was working in a job where the level of disrespect toward patients was intolerable. It's one thing to stay silent when the problems seem too big, too systemic and too 'high up the ladder' to be tackled effectively, but when you see a person's basic human rights violated without cause, it makes you evaluate things in a very different light. Have the medical and nursing professions in Ireland become so pragmatic and so cynical that all we now care about is advancing our careers and receiving our pay cheque at the end of the month? In that job, I saw the basic foundations of good medical practice ripped apart on a daily basis, and I came to the point where I was no longer able to tolerate it. Yet, I felt I could do nothing, change nothing, because I was trapped within a system where wanting change, demanding change, marks you out as a troublemaker. But what I began to realise was that the biggest problem with the health service was the lack of candid information available to the public about its failures. It was then I decided that if nothing else, I could at least help to raise awareness around the issues.

My idealistic motive is tempered by a good dose of realism. Writing this book has not been an easy process and I am under no illusions regarding the possible consequences of my actions. I have known doctors whose careers have been jeopardised as a result of speaking out about bad practice in the workplace. What, then, might be the consequence of opening a dialogue with the entire Irish public? I am in no doubt that were my identity to be revealed, it would greatly diminish my future prospects and possibly even force me to go to another country if I want to continue practising medicine. Indeed, even my own unreservedly supportive family – a number of whom are in the medical profession – have repeatedly expressed concerns about my writing this book.

But while I come to it with my eyes wide open, I can no longer stand idly by and watch the simple things ignored, watch patients, nurses and doctors pay the price for bad policies that serve the interests of everyone but the public. In this, I am an idealist. I write this in the hope that some members of the public will know more about the problems facing the health service, so that when they discuss it with their friends, or lobby their local TDs, they will have the necessary information to hand. My hope is that when people read this account, they will feel the same anger and indignation I felt when confronted by the poor parody of efficiency that is the Irish health service. I know change, whenever it does come, will come dropping slow, but at least by writing this book I can wake up in the morning, look in the mirror and not lie to myself. And if there is a price to be paid for throwing back the veil and revealing the truth as best I can, it cannot be greater than that intangible price a human pays when he does nothing in the face of suffering. People deserve to know: it is their tax money after all. *The Bitter Pill* is one doctor's attempt to inform people of the key issues that plague the health services from the inside. Perhaps together we can identify and take responsibility for the malignant precursors in the bloodstream of our health body, and then devise the social and political vaccines necessary to eradicate them. This is not a witch-hunt, however, nor should it be. The problems lie not so much with individuals as with a system that is deeply flawed. With this in mind, I have concealed names, places and exact times, where appropriate. These details are not necessary for the incidents I discuss because, unfortunately, none of these incidents are isolated.

Chapter 1

Overview: Broken Parts

The widespread crisis that is crippling A&E departments throughout Ireland is essentially the focal point of the entire malaise: every aspect of medicine and healthcare feeds into A&E, which means it has become the repository of all the problems of the health system at large. In order to understand the nature and extent of the A&E crisis, it is therefore necessary to examine each constituent broken part, each system and each service, because they all contribute to the whole, weakening it and straining it ever closer to breaking point. For the patient, in the end it all boils down to one intractable fact: interminable waiting times, often on trolleys, for those who enter any of the country's A&E departments.

THE TWO-TIER SYSTEM

No discussion of the Irish health system can take place without an examination of its foundations. It is built on the two-tier system of public and private healthcare. At the heart of this system is a blatant lie about choice, one that is propagated by the government and by all vested interests in a health system that rewards private practice and penalises public patients. The two-tier system is the single greatest obstacle to improving the level of health care provided in this country. This is because it leeches off resources paid for by the tax-payer and gives little in return to the public, while providing incentives to doctors to neglect their public duties. As such, it is a system that serves no one other than those who profit from it, and it works fundamentally against the improvement of public health services. Yet as long as this system prevails, those who can afford to rightly feel they have little choice but to purchase private healthcare.

THE POWER OF CONSULTANTS

The two-tier system, in turn, must be understood in terms of the role of consultants and, more specifically, the power they wield within the health service. Consultants are paid by the State to work a normal working day in their public capacity, but they retain complete discretion over when they choose to be in the hospital and when they choose to leave. Consultants who complain about having to work long hours often neglect to mention that many of those hours are spent looking after their private patients to supplement their income. Considering that the Irish tax-payer is paying salaries upwards of €140k per annum to these men and women, there is a major question to be asked about accountability.

It is a well-established and universally accepted fact that accountability is a key factor in achieving the standards of best medical practice. 'Measuring practice' and comparing it 'against existing standards' are key components in the audit cycle, the gold-standard for evaluating and improving medical practice. Yet in the 'Medical Consultants Report', published in March 2007 by the Comptroller and Auditor General, it was found that no record is kept of how many hours consultants devote to public service as compared to private work, and that the prioritising of private patients is leading to a neglect of public care.

There is also a lack of impartial oversight of their activities. For example, most departments are required to have routine morbidity and mortality meetings to discuss the problems that have occurred in treating patients. But there is no external observer present. Furthermore, the presentations are prepared by the consultant's team and are reviewed by the consultant prior to being shown to anyone outside the team. The result is that mistakes made by the consultant are unlikely to be high-lighted. Greater accountability and oversight are not to be scoffed at. Consultants who are above critic-ism and above correction will make more mistakes, and those mistakes are likely to accumulate with time. The smaller, daily, unnoticed mistakes will delay recovery and impact the health service negat-ively without ever coming to the forefront.

The reality is that consultants have the power to set their own rules, and there is no one to challenge them. Junior doctors, though well placed to observe wrong-doing and abuses of power, are imprisoned in silence by fear. A single reference from a consult-ant is enough to make or break their careers. The fact that the only group of people able to observe and understand the mistakes of consultants are unable to speak out allows an attitude of arrogance to prevail. This culture of fear makes change for the better all the more difficult to achieve.

RADIOLOGY

Radiology is the nexus of the health service. In order for a decision to be reached about a patient's treatment, regardless of whether the illness is medical or surgical, routine scans and x-rays are needed. If the radiology service is not running smoothly, it creates a trickle-down effect in the treatment of patients in every other specialty. One of the biggest factors directly influencing the length of in-patient stays is the waiting list for scans. Delays in scanning and reporting results create a delay in treatment, which in turn means a delay in discharge. This is linked closely with the two-tier system and the role of consultants.

Imagine a radiologist's office. On his desk sit two stacks of x-rays. One stack, usually the bigger one, is that of public patients; the other is that of private patients. For each private x-ray the radiologist will be paid upwards of €50. For the public x-rays he has already been paid, in his monthly salary. Whether the public x-ray is reported on today, tomorrow or next week, the radiologist will still be paid the full amount of his salary, on time. For private scans, on the other hand, he will be paid only after he has completed them. The upshot is that the private scans often take precedence over the public ones.

The situation has now become so dire that often by the time a routine x-ray of a public patient has been reported, the patient has already been discharged. More often, though, it leads to unnecessary prolonged hospital stays, which lengthens the waiting time for those lying on A&E trolleys.

We need to offer a modern, standardised and efficient radiology service. Scans and reports on scans should be available twenty-four hours a day. We will return to this issue later to see how these improvements can be achieved.

HYGIENE

Poor hygiene has a stark impact on hospital beds. Outbreaks of MRSA and other hospital-acquired infections not only affect the patients who suffer at their hands but severely affect the number of free beds by prolonging the hospital stays of those patients who contracted the virus. This represents a waste of resources. A patient who acquires an infection needs to be treated and investigated, which increases the cost of the in-patient stay. Between the cost of blood tests, antibiotics, man hours of nurses, doctors and other hospital staff and of keeping a bed occupied in the acute hospital, it adds up to a considerable waste of tax-payers' money. All of this unnecessary waste is often simply the result of a lack of proper basic hygiene on the part of hospital professionals. Clearly, facilitating and encouraging good hygiene should be top of the agenda.

WORKING CONDITIONS

In order to have good hygiene and an efficient

health service, we first need to ensure that all hospital staff are provided with optimum working conditions. Within the hospital hierarchy, this need is most pressing for junior doctors. The truth is that fatigue leads to mistakes – and junior doctors regularly suffer from extreme fatigue. While major catastrophes as a result of this are, thankfully, rare, minor incidents occur so routinely that they have almost become an acceptable part of daily life in a hospital. If doctors are to provide care at the highest level, they need to have normal working hours and rest breaks. This is crucial for the future of the health system.

NURSING HOME PLACEMENT CRISIS
If all patients awaiting placement in nursing homes could be provided with a nursing-home bed right this minute, it would free up enough beds to seriously reduce the A&E crisis. It is a shocking statistic. Hospitals are not nursing homes and should not be used as such. The blame for this must be laid at the door of the government, which is not fulfilling its responsibility to provide appropriate care for the elderly.

MENTAL HEALTH
One in four people in Ireland has suffered from depression at some point in their lives, yet the plight

of the mentally ill is bottom of the health agenda. While this problem is not directly related to the A&E crisis, there is no one out there who does not have a family member, friend or acquaintance who hasn't paid the price for the poor standard of mental health services in Ireland.

RACISM

Racism has profound implications for the functioning of our health service. What is rarely stated overtly, but is nevertheless true, is that discrimination on the basis of race is rife within the Irish health system. Promotion and advancement are largely the preserve of white doctors. Overseas medics continually come up against a brick wall when it comes to career advancement. In an age where more and more doctors are coming from outside Ireland to work here, this issue is of increasing importance.

SYSTEMS OF EMPLOYMENT

If we do not employ the best doctors for the job, if we allow personal preference, favouritism, background or personal connections to be primary deciding factors, then how can the patient receive the best possible care? Until and unless doctors can be selected fairly and impartially, without prejudice, the system simply cannot operate to best effect.

DOCUMENTATION

Medical documentation is the recording and preservation of the medical history of the patient. This includes details of current illness, past ailments, as well as treatment and investigations to date. Poor documentation at hospitals, clinics, hostels and nursing homes is a major cause of delay as it creates paper trails that are cumbersome and awkward.

We need to overhaul our method of storing information and our method of accessing it. Medical notes and other information should be made available, without delay, to professionals treating our patients. A nationwide network of health services data will not only allow better treatment but also better oversight and auditing of the services being provided, so that they can be examined critically and improved.

NURSING

There are many problems with the way nursing in Ireland is being managed. Nurses are being prevented from doing their jobs efficiently by pointless protocols and rigid management. Many face 'burn out' and gross disillusionment as the realities of the system wear down their ideals and the caring instinct that brought them into the profession in the first place. The result is compromised patient care.

The hierarchy that exists in hospitals also affects how nurses do their jobs. Where roles are not defined clearly, tensions can arise between staff members, which can create an unpleasant working environment. This also compromises the position and role of nurses.

THE PUBLIC'S ROLE IN IMPROVING THE HEALTH SYSTEM

The health service exists to serve the public. It follows that the public must be part of the solution. That's you. You have a responsibility to ask questions and to raise the issues. If things are not to your satisfaction, you must point it out and make your voice heard. To this end, let me share a secret with you: verbal complaints are a waste of time. Written complaints, on the other hand, get noticed. You will be surprised just how many wheels can be pushed into motion by a brief letter to the right people.

The days of 'no-questions-asked' are over. If you witness something that disturbs you, for example in the area of hospital hygiene or patient care, or find yourself or your loved one in an unsatisfactory position, interminably waiting for a public appointment, don't stand idly by or feel powerless. Raise your voice, lobby your local TD, use the airwaves, do whatever you need to do to get noticed. Make a case for change.

NUMBER-CRUNCHING

The one issue I have not yet touched upon is perhaps the most pressing problem of all: there are not enough doctors and there are not enough beds. In this regard the government has failed spectacularly. But while we wait for the government to wake up to this bigger picture and address the needs of a rapidly growing population, efficiency needs to be restored.

These, then, are the broken parts that must be fixed if our health service is to operate fairly, efficiently and for the good of all patients. The mistake many commentators make is to point to one specific area and exclaim, 'If only this were put right, then everything else would fall into place.' That is an extremely myopic view of the problem. In truth, we need to examine the cause and effects of each of these problems before we can begin to tease out a solution. And that solution must, of necessity, be a multifaceted approach to cross-the-board improvements, revisions and wholesale changes.

Chapter 2

The Two-tier System of Healthcare

In order that a private health service can justify its existence, it is necessary that it offers a better service than the public health service. It follows, then, that the public service is below-par and therefore unable to deliver best practice. I believe that there are several ways in which the two-tier system is partially and directly responsible for the current crisis in the health service. Primarily, these are: the issue of incentive – strong financial motivations for consultants to prioritise private work over their public duty; consultants dividing their time disproportionately between public and private duties – the use of resources, investment and the myth of choice.

THE ISSUE OF INCENTIVE

Here is a common story: my patient was recovering very well from his recent illness and today was finally fit enough to go home. He himself wanted to go home, was looking forward to it and, as is almost always the case, his bed was needed for someone in the long line of patients waiting in A&E. He was not discharged for a further day. The reason for the delay was that my patient needed to see the consultant prior to being discharged, and the consultant was not around that day. Unfortunately, this is a daily occurrence: not a single day goes by in an Irish hospital when one patient, or more, is kept on unnecessarily because the consultant is unavailable to discharge him.

Why is this so often the case? In addition to their public health duties, many consultants also do private work that regularly takes them away from the hospital in which they work. They are in no way held to account in this respect. In fact, there is even disagreement on the exact number of hours consultants are required to devote to public duty under their current contract. According to the report published in 2007 by the Comptroller and Auditor General:

> The HSE claims that 39 hours per week, inclusive of six hours of unschedulable

activities, is provided for, while the consultants contend that a 33 hour week is what was contracted for. It is disappointing that this matter has not been resolved in the ten years since the contract was signed in 1997.

Once there is no major mishap with patients and no one is getting sued, the HSE seems happy to turn a blind eye to consultants' attendance. This gives consultants an unjustifiable carte blanche in terms of their working schedule. While flexibility can be a good thing, it is not the same as being able to decide what one's obligations should be. Even the Irish Medical Organisation (IMO) agrees with the Auditor's report that current practices are insufficient and unreliable as a means of documenting whether or not consultants are discharging their contracted public commitments. An IMO press release in 2007 said of the report: 'It also highlights the need for verification systems, which the IMO supports,' going on to claim that in its opinion the verification would show that consultants worked more than the prescribed hours.

So, for the well and waiting public patient, unwittingly holding up a much-needed bed, what happens when the consultant is not available? It is true that, in some cases, the consultant can plan a discharge in advance, instructing the medical team to discharge the patient the following day, or the day after, if certain pre-defined conditions are met. Another option is to receive the consultant's consent to discharge over the phone. However, while consultants do make themselves available on the phone, it is usually reserved for cases of a serious emergency only. Unfortunately, a patient who is well and awaiting discharge is not considered an emergency situation. In fact, this situation occurs so often that telephoning the consultant each time consent was needed would quickly become a serious annoyance.

Occasionally a consultant will trust his/her registrar sufficiently to permit the registrar to make the decision regarding a patient. This is a relatively rare occurrence, however, as the consultant is ultimately responsible and it takes a long time to establish that level of trust and faith in the ability of colleagues. As most registrar jobs in the country are one-year long, many months can pass before the relationship is solid enough for such liberties, and soon thereafter the process begins anew.

So what happens with our well and waiting patient? More often than not, he is simply left waiting until the consultant does his next public round.

It returns us to the question of working hours and accountability. The key issue to consider here is incentive. Consultants, like the rest of us, are human beings, and they respond to incentives the same way anyone else would. What exactly is the incentive for consultants to stay in their public role from 9.00am to 5.00pm when they can devote time to a highly lucrative private practice? The two-tier system provides a massive incentive for consultants to be less devoted to their public sector duties than they might otherwise be. Yet the cost to the Irish economy of facilitating, and arguably fostering, private practice is incalculable.

The solution is to create a system where there is an incentive to do the public job. The new consultant contracts are a step in the right direction, but it has to be done sensibly. Right now consultants earn a public salary ranging anywhere from €120,000 to over €200,000 per annum. Consultants can make more than double this from private practice alone; earnings in excess of €400,000–€500,000 are not uncommon, and in many cases much higher.

The initial amount offered to consultants for working exclusively in the public sector was around €220,000 per annum. If the government was at all serious about convincing consultants to do public work exclusively, then this was a ludicrous idea. What person in their right mind would voluntarily take such a massive pay cut? The government needs to adopt a more realistic approach in its future negotiations if definite progress is to be made. We need to change the lure of financial incentive to pull consultants towards public duty rather than pushing them towards private work. Aside from this, no public contract is meaningful without robust monitoring and enforcement of agreed contractual obligations – just as exists for any public servant.

THE MYTH OF CHOICE

A friend of mine, who is a consultant, used to work in the NHS in the UK. His first two children were born in the UK and throughout both pregnancies his wife did not need to make use of private health services. The NHS took good care of her, and as a couple they were very happy with the level of service provided. Once they relocated to Ireland, however, they felt compelled to take out private health cover for the birth of their next child.

It is very difficult to comprehend what it is like to be a pregnant woman in the Irish public health service unless you work in the system, or have been a client of it. There is the endless, intolerable waiting in over-crowded reception areas, exacerbated by fatigue and backache. At the end of that wait, the woman may end up being seen in the main by a medical student or junior doctor. As a medical student I saw pregnant patients with only a nurse as chaperone. I'd then report my findings to the consultant, who rarely spent more than a minute or two with each patient. When it comes to labour, the consultant may or may have been available.

For private patients, the experience is very different, from pregnancy to delivery. During the final stage, the consultant is available for the delivery, night or day.

We are told that the reason for the two-tier system is patient choice. This is a myth. Those who cannot afford private healthcare don't have a choice, while those who can afford it feel forced into opting for it – hardly a choice either. Public or private, what woman or couple doesn't want the reassurance of a fully trained consultant during the delivery process? Is it acceptable to say that public patients don't have a right to, or don't deserve the same level of, safety and reassurance? No, it is not acceptable, but that is exactly what is happening.

It's not hard to see why mothers-to-be and families who can afford it almost always 'choose' to go private. If we view public and private healthcare as brands, it is clear that, even if the basic model is the same, one brand offers a better quality of service. If the public health system provided the high standards of care, efficiency and courtesy accepted in medical science, then would you pay extra for a private service? The difference we are talking about is not extra bells and whistles, it is the basic service that ought to be provided. When the issue is health, most people don't want choice, they want reliable, standardised care. They want to be treated as well and as quickly as possible and to be relieved of their symptoms. Public health care has a duty to meet that minimum standard of care, yet it fails to, despite the fact that our taxes pay for it and entitle us to it.

What is presented to us as a choice is, in fact, no choice at all. Though no one is forcing us to take out health insurance and we can choose not to, there may be negative consequences of doing so, for example, longer waiting times for appointments and treatment. Many people will be aware of Susie Long, or 'Rosie' as she was first known, the brave woman whose story was told after she wrote to RTÉ Radio 1's 'Liveline' programme early in 2007.* Her cancer diagnosis came too late for the treatment that would have significantly increased her chances of survival. Why? Because she was on a lengthy waiting list for a routine test, during which time the cancer spread until it was diagnosed incurable. Did Susie Long have a choice? Is it her fault that the health service failed to deliver this basic service on an urgent basis? It's a slippery slope. Once you start apologising and making excuses for charging

*See Appendix, p. 251, for the transcript of Susie Long's eloquent and moving letter describing her story.

money to provide basic healthcare, it is inevitable that tragedy will follow.

What it has come to now is that we have a health service that values the health and life of the private patient over that of the public patient: a system of apartheid at the heart of Ireland's health system. Public patients who need critical care, whose lives are in danger, will get the help they need. But those who are not obviously dying are expected to suffer. The truth is that waiting lists are no longer a head-turning issue in this country. Everyone knows that the waiting lists are long, everyone knows that people are suffering while they are waiting, but we have become apathetic about this because it is the norm. It takes someone being diagnosed with terminal cancer to make us even raise our eyebrows, to look and take notice, to say that, yes, maybe something is not right here.

This is the myth of choice: pay up, or suffer. It's your choice.

But what if the public health service were running smoothly? What if people got seen within a week, or two weeks, of being referred to a specialist by their GP? What if the standard of care was of a level that we have a right to expect in a First World country with one of the strongest economies in Europe. What then? Would anyone pay for a few extras provided by private health insurance? Maybe a few would opt to do so, but certainly not the 50 per cent that currently choose this alternative. This is the crux of the problem, the cause and the symptom: private healthcare can exist only as long as the public service is unacceptable to a large section of our population. It is therefore in the interests of all those who profit from it, all those who lobby the government to invest in it, that the public health service in Ireland remains at a lower standard. Serious improvement in the public health service would clearly result in a downturn in the private health market – hardly an incentive for the powers-that-be to argue for radical change.

Another myth of choice revolves around the debate concerning competition in health insurance. Many people are under the misguided belief that competition among insurance companies drives prices down. In fact, the opposite is the case.

Take the hypothetical situation where only one insurance company operates in the market. A consultant sets a price on his private service, then enters into negotiation with the insurance company. If the consultant refuses to negotiate or makes unreasonable demands, the insurance company can threaten not to pay for his service. After all, there are plenty of other consultants to work with. This forces consultants, radiologists and private hospitals to negotiate and offer more reasonable terms to the health insurance company, which cost-saving can be passed on to the consumer.

A second insurance company opens for business, and now the consultant has options. He sets his price and negotiates with the old company and the new one. This works out very well for him because the competition is no longer between private services providers, now it is between the two companies who are vying for business. Naturally, the consultant prefers to see the patients of the company that offers him a better deal. This raises the cost of everything for the insurance companies, and this extra cost is passed on to the consumer in the form of higher premiums.

The mantra that choice is good is not always applicable when it comes to health issues.

THE PROBLEM WITH WAITING LISTS

Waiting lists create many problems because it means people get sicker while waiting to be assessed and treated. Unfortunately, it is in the interest of many consultants that this situation remain unresolved. I don't suggest that consultants are intentionally making the situation bad so that they can profit from the misery of others, but it is blatantly obvious that there is very little incentive for consultants to be pro-active in helping to fix these problems. Hiring more consultants will help, but a radical alteration of the administrative system will be a necessary long-term solution. As long as private and public healthcare operates as it currently does, the public health service will never operate fully in the patients' interests.

THE LEECHING OF RESOURCES

According to an OECD report published in 2004, health insurance covers 49 per cent of the Irish population. This means that almost half of the people attending the A&E department in public hospitals have private health insurance. Is this because private hospitals don't have enough beds? No. It is because private hospitals are set up to engage in activities that are profitable. A&E is not profitable.

Performing pre-planned procedures, such as scans, tests and even operations, is profitable. The patient is admitted, the job is done and the patient is discharged within a couple of days. The cost of this to the hospital is minimal, but it charges a premium for the procedures. Providing an A&E service, on the hand, means dealing with minor illnesses and injuries, looking after patients who are admitted for a prolonged period of time, providing rehabilitation services, physiotherapists, occupational therapists and intensive-care units. None of this is profitable.

In other words, private hospitals need public

hospitals to fulfil certain key functions. Patients who have complications after private procedures or who need long recovery periods are often cared for in public hospitals. The downside of this is that it means the private hospitals are using the public hospitals' nursing, administrative and medical staff to look after their patients, whilst bearing none of the cost. This in turn means that resources, including consultants' time, are being drained from the public sector to facilitate the greater efficiency of the private sector.

The government has proposed to tackle the bed crisis by building private hospitals on public grounds. This 'co-location' proposal will, it is said, create 1,000 extra beds. The implication is that those extra beds will free up a corresponding number of beds for public patients. But this is just smoke and mirrors. There is no shortage of beds in private hospitals – as is evident by the lack of waiting lists in those institutions. Providing more beds may provide more profit, but it will do little to ease the pressure of the current crisis. The central problem will still remain, which is that we are in a situation where it is accepted that people are charged extra for something they have already paid for through their taxes. The artificially created necessity for private healthcare is driven by profit, at the expense of patients.

Chapter 3

The Consultant Dilemma

There are two pressing questions in relation to consultants: do they have too much power and is that power dangerous for the patients under their care? In order to light on this subject, I will relate an incident that occurred while I was working as a non-consultant hospital doctor (NCHD) in surgery.

I was attached to a Urology consultant during my surgical rotation. This consultant, a well-trained and highly regarded surgeon for whom I have the utmost respect, has a reputation for efficiency and providing an exceptionally high standard of care. Sadly, one black mark blots this memory. On this particular day, it was early in the morning and he was on a whirlwind ward round, his team scampering behind him. One of the patients we were due to see was a young man who had been admitted the night before. He had come in with severe testicular pain and had had emergency exploratory surgery. Luckily, he did not have a torsion of his testis and was due to be discharged the following morning.

The consultant saw him on the ward round and peeled back the dressing to examine the wound. He was quite vigorous and hasty in his technique. The patient was visibly in a great deal of pain and gave a muffled yell. The consultant replaced the bandage and continued on his rounds. Less than an hour later I was called by concerned nursing staff; the patient was bleeding. I arrived on the ward to find the young man in severe, intractable pain and bleeding profusely from the site of the surgery. His wound had 'dihessed', or come apart. We had to apply strong and constant pressure to stave the bleeding, but the pain was uncontrollable, even with a massive dose of intra-muscular pethidine on top of the regular analgesia he was already receiving. He had to be taken to theatre for emergency surgery within the hour. I gasped in shock and horror as the consultant jokingly chastised him before the surgery. 'You weren't pulling at the wound, were you?' he asked.

The man was very fortunate in that he escaped any long-term complications. He was able to go home a couple of days later and remained well. But, he might easily have ended up losing one or both testicles, with all the associated complications. The NCHD's on the team were all of the opinion that the complication was a result of the consultant's brusque manner. Yet none of us complained, spoke a single word or voiced any form of protest. Why? We were afraid. Ultimately, no harm had been done and the patient recovered, and thus we soothed our consciences. We all needed references at the end of the job, and we all knew that taking on a consultant is literally career suicide. When those higher up the ladder wield that kind of power, it can have an adverse effect on colleagues and patients alike.

Balancing Power and responsibility

Consultants are burdened with a unique responsibility that no other profession in the world can equal: they deal in life and death. Their decisions and actions impact not just individuals but families and communities. In an age when litigation is rising, that responsibility can have very grave consequences indeed. Arguably, it has resulted in the practice of a very defensive medicine, i.e. treatment that may not necessarily be the most efficient and beneficial, but is the least likely to attract law suits.

Additionally, we live in an increasingly volatile environment, in which trust has been eroded. People no longer take their doctor's word on faith, perhaps rightly so. Internet access and the ready availability of huge amounts of information on all topics, albeit often unsubstantiated, does not make matters any easier. Self-diagnosis is on the increase. Patients often turn up to a clinic having already decided what their illness is, what the treatment should be and how long it will take for them to get better. When the clinical reality varies from their expectations, this can have a negative effect not only on the patient's state of mind but also on their compliance with the prescribed treatment.

As so much responsibility lies on the shoulders of so few men and women, it is right, and also essential, that they have a measure of power to enable them to carry out their tasks. However, with any power comes the possibility of abuse, and that requires vigilance and strict parameters of work and practice.

So, where does a consultant's power come from? First there are the various boards, committees and interview panels on which consultants sit. The 1997 consultants' contract provided for the creation of management boards, with consultant representation, to run each hospital. Consultants also sit on the interview panels that appoint not only junior doctors and specialist registrars but also other consultants. This means they have a lot of influence in deciding who is appointed under them. They can, with a single letter, make or break a doctor's career. For example, one consultant in a Dublin hospital is known for his ability to get people who have worked under him as registrars onto the specialist registrar scheme, if he likes them. These positions – the first step towards an eventual consultancy – are few and far between and extremely coveted.

A consultant also has a lot of leverage in deciding clinics and how they are run. He can, for example, move a patient up or down the list at his discretion; the same goes for operations or investigative procedures. Recently a friend of a consultant was admitted to a hospital under my team. This was a time when we, as a team, were struggling with huge delays for certain types of radiology scan due to an extensive waiting list. In this case, it was also affecting private patients. A quick phone call between one consultant and another resulted in the friend having the investigation completed, reported and being discharged from the hospital on the same day. Unlike those gathered in A&E, he didn't have to wait for four hours to be seen and then spend eight hours on a trolley before being allocated a bed. This is a common enough practice in medicine, and is considered a professional courtesy that doctors extend to one other. When it gets extended on to friends, too, it becomes more questionable. Consultants are also frequently involved in how funds received from their local HSE are spent. Does this affect the treatment of patients and the Irish tax-payer?

Let's take the case of Dr Michael Neary, the disgraced gynaecologist from Our Lady of Lourdes Hospital in Drogheda, who was found to have performed scores of unjustifiable hysterectomies. Eventually, it was a midwife who blew the whistle on his practice. Surely at least some doctors working under him over the years had noticed something was amiss – why did they not speak out? The answer is simple: fear. You do not embarrass or correct someone with the power to destroy your career on a whim. You certainly cannot go up against a consultant, and why would you? You are undertaking a six-month rotation, while the consultant has been, and will be, there for years, so who is going to believe you? And where will the reference for your next job come from? These are the kinds of thoughts that make us stifle our conscience and get on with the job, which allows the cycle of power and abuse of power to continue unchecked.

Unfortunately, precedent shows that those who dare to challenge the power of consultants, for whatever reason, often find themselves stranded, with nowhere to turn. Some real-life incidents are the best way to illustrate this.

The first relates to a young doctor working in a

training scheme involving several hospitals, some Dublin-based and a few from outside the county. He was chosen as a representative by his fellow trainees at one of the hospitals for an annual meeting with the scheme tutor. At the meeting they had a very pleasant and friendly conversation. The tutor asked him about the training at the hospital and his views on it. He replied that he found it to be of a very high standard. Further on in the conversation, the tutor asked if there were any concerns. The trainee pointed out an issue that his colleagues had requested he bring up, should the opportunity arise. Some of the overseeing bodies' recommendations for training in that branch required trainees to be instructed in certain techniques. He pointed out to the scheme tutor, a consultant, that the consultants at his hospitals did not know how to perform those techniques. How could they adequately train him and his colleagues in accordance with the overseeing bodies' instructions? The consultant agreed that this was a matter for concern and thanked him for bringing it to his attention on behalf of the other trainees. He promised to look at the issue in greater depth.

A few days later the trainee received a letter informing him that his position on the scheme had become untenable and he had been terminated. When he questioned this decision, he was politely informed that the decision was final and had been arrived at because he had been overly critical of his supervising consultants.

This young doctor did manage to find another job, but that was the end of the progress of his career. He later sat a diploma exam, in which he was successful. But he found out subsequently that he had narrowly missed being failed because a letter had been written to the diploma committee declaring that, while the candidate was a good doctor, he had a personality incompatible with his profession. This letter was shown to him by a bewildered examiner, who could find absolutely nothing wrong with the candidate, his knowledge or his behaviour during the examination.

This same doctor has since been failed on several consecutive occasions while trying to pass the overseeing college's professional exam for that specialty. Most of the time he has failed the oral exams, not the written ones, even though other consultants with whom he has worked have spoken highly of his skills and expertise. In fact, in hospitals he which he has worked, this doctor has been asked to instruct other doctors and nurses in the correct performance of the very skills he is repeatedly failed on during oral exams. He is considered good enough by various authorities to teach these skills, but not good enough to pass the exams testing these talents.

His consultants are confused as to how such a

dedicated, experienced and knowledgable candidate can repeatedly fail an exam that should be simple for someone of his calibre. Upon making enquiries to the college concerned, the initial reply he received was that perhaps these examinations were not a true reflection of clinical skill and he was simply unfortunate and unlucky. More than half a dozen times?

Further probing by consultants sympathetic to his cause revealed, strictly off the record, that occasionally the college did 'flag' certain candidates – read 'blacklist' – deemed for one reason or another as unsuitable to continue a career in said specialty. The hope was that after failing two or three times (and spending a lot of money on exam fees and a lot of time and energy studying), the candidate would become disheartened and give up.

The doctor was distraught to learn this and hired a solicitor. Through his solicitor he sent a letter to the college, asking them if there were such a bar on him and requesting all personal information related to him in their files. He is legally entitled to this information under the Freedom of Information Act. The college replied that, yes, he was entitled to the information and they would be more than happy to hand it over. This gesture was not without caveats, however. The small print, spotted by the lawyer, pointed out that during the investigation of his case, while the matter was being resolved, he would not be allowed to sit any exams. Furthermore, regardless of the findings of the college, it would have the right to bar him from the exam. He was requested to sign a document agreeing to these conditions before any further information would be released.

This clever ploy of blackmail worked: who would take the risk, however slim, that they might just have been unlucky thus far and perhaps will pass the next time, rather than being barred from ever sitting the exam again? The doctor is currently studying for his eleventh attempt and has thus far passed the theory section. Bear in mind that this same college has in the past openly acknowledged that it had wrongly failed a candidate through incorrect marking. Despite admitting this, the college refused to pass the candidate. Such unfair, not to mention illegal, practices keep junior doctors in constant fear of reprisals, rendering them powerless to act.

As we know, there is little protection for whistleblowers in Ireland, not just in medicine but across the board. This one of the biggest reasons why it took so long for Doctor Neary's 'mistakes' to come to light. Yet, instead of promoting transparency and encouraging whistleblowers, Minister for Health Mary Harney is trying her best to further copper fasten this lack of accountability to patients of the health service. This is evident in one of the clauses included in the proposed new consultant contract. According to the IMO website: "The contract does not contain an acceptable advocacy clause and would prevent Consultants advocating publicly where it could be shown that those comments adversely affect the reputation of the hospital and the morale of staff in the hospital."

So forget about junior doctors, even consultants are going to be gagged from pointing out problems in the hospital, if it is deemed to bring the hospital into disrepute or effect staff morale. And who exactly gets to decide when this is the case? No doubt the HSE, and the managers working in that hospital, whose mistakes might be highlighted by whistleblowing. Since when did the person who committed the wrongdoing get to decide whether or not that wrongdoing should be exposed? While the Irish government is openly apologising to patients for mistakes of the past, it is simultaneously paving the way for future mistakes by advocating such a clause.

The second incident concerns a young junior doctor who has also been working in Ireland for several years. One weekday morning his wife, who is his only relative living in Ireland, fell ill and he was forced to take her to the A&E. He was scheduled to be on call from 9.30am, so he rang the hospital before that time to inform them of his present situation. A few minutes later he received a phone call from the covering consultant, who sharply informed him that it was his responsibility to organise for someone to cover him and that if he couldn't do so, he must return to his post immediately. The doctor again explained his situation, but the consultant remained unmoved.

The doctor then rang the other junior doctors on duty that day and asked them to help him out. It was only a matter of someone holding the pager for three or four hours because another doctor had agreed to cover him from 1.00pm. No one was in a position to help him, so he was forced to ring the consultant again and tell him that he had been unable to arrange cover.

The consultant's response was that he didn't care, that it was his responsibility and that if he didn't return straight away, he would be forced to take up the matter with the hospital director. The doctor had no choice: he was forced to return to work, not knowing how serious was the condition of his wife nor whether she needed his assistance.

Thankfully, his wife came through unscathed. The next day the consultant concerned approached him and apologised. Thus the doctor felt the matter was resolved. However, a month later, when the time came to renew his position, he was not shortlisted for interview, despite being one of the most experienced candidates. The available posts were given to candidates more junior than him.

The final incident I will relate is perhaps the most disturbing because it shows that even senior doctors are not always protected when they speak openly.

A specialist registrar in Obstetrics and Gynaecology was asked to fill out an anonymous and confidential survey on the training she was receiving en route to accreditation for consultancy. This she did to the best of her ability. Her only criticism was that she hadn't had the opportunity to practice a certain surgical procedure mandated as necessary by the Royal College of Obstetricians and Gynaecologists. She felt she needed more supervised training so that she would be fully proficient in this technique when performing it solo.

This doctor had been getting on very well with her consultants up to that point. At each quarterly assessment, which was a feature of her training, she had received glowing reviews. However, just weeks after she had submitted this 'confidential and anonymous' survey, her assessment changed dramatically. She had gone from being a model trainee and top-notch consultant material to being someone who did not get along well with patients and staff, according to her supervising consultants. She tried to contest this assessment, but ran into a brick wall. Her next two assessments were due from the same consultants and continued failure would mean the end of her career.

Realising that she had made some powerful enemies, she had to act swiftly and decisively to save her career. She resigned her post immediately and found herself a job, without pay, in a different constituency, where she was not known. She worked hard and quietly for the duration and earned a glowing reference from her consultants there, which allowed her to resume her training. But the cost was high. She had had to sacrifice over a year of accredited training and had nearly witnessed her career destroyed for daring to suggest that the training she was receiving was not adequate *per* the Royal College's guidelines for an upcoming consultant. The powers-that-be would rather have an under-trained consultant than cause mild embarrassment to the supervising consultants at the training centre.

Given all this – the power consultants wield within the hospital hierarchy and the occasionally questionable nature of the training imparted to trainees – it makes one wonder if there are more Michael Nearys waiting in the wings.

Sadly, the people who are best placed to spot such problems and act as a check against them are junior doctors. They work very closely with their consultants and have an in-depth knowledge and understanding of their practices and patient-management strategies. Consequently, they can quickly recognise inconsistencies and problems. But they are in the worst possible position to be able to point out such problems, or to do anything about them.

Most good consultants will openly admit that there is much they do not know. In fact, the best consultants in the country are often those who are most humble in the face of their own knowledge because medicine is a vast subject and one that is constantly growing. There isn't a single consultant practising today who doesn't espouse the virtues of honesty and forthrightness. 'Always tell us if there is a problem. Don't hesitate,' is the mantra that is oft recited.

The reality is different, however, as one surgical registrar told me as he reprimanded me for asking too many questions. 'Consultants don't want smart juniors. They want someone who will do the job quickly, quietly and efficiently without asking too many questions and in a way that will cause the minimum fuss for them.'

The truth is that the fine ideals that are fêted the loudest in public are rarely followed in practice. This has an impact not only in terms of checks and balances and the ability of junior doctors to function adequately but also, more directly, on patient care. In the large Dublin hospitals, junior doctors on-call can generally rely on advice and support from someone more senior if they are unsure as to the best management options for their patient. This is not necessarily the case in smaller hospitals outside Dublin, where, depending on the specialty involved, often the only person a junior doctor can consult in times of doubt is the covering consultant. Although the standard advice doled out in medical school is 'when in doubt, call your consultant, regardless of what time of day or night', it often does not pan out this way in practice. In fact, one purveyor of this advice gave short shrift to a junior doctor when he needed assistance. 'But you have disturbed me!' the consultant fumed. Another doctor in a similar situation was told, 'You should be able to handle this by now. What are you ringing me for?' This brusque manner is part of a general attitude that discourages junior doctors from seeking help.

In the main, consultants are genuine, caring people, who joined this profession to help others, not simply to make money, and I believe that this is still at the heart of their day-to-day work. They are still human, though, when all is said and done, which means they can fall prey to a 'god complex' if given total control. The current system is flawed in their favour: it allows individuals to cover up their mistakes, while preventing others from speaking out when things are not right. It is essential that a balance is struck: that consultants have enough power to do their jobs well, but not so much power that they answer to no one but themselves.

Chapter 4

Radiology:
The Broken Cog in the Machine

Radiology is the apparatus that keeps the whole machine moving. It is a vital ingredient in the management of almost every single patient. No matter what the specialty, Radiology will have a role to play. Radiology departments are responsible for x-rays when you break a bone, or have a chest infection or other lung disease, or even stomach problems. They scan patients for evidence of early cancer and in determination of the extent of late cancer. Radiology provides us with a bird's-eye view of the problem, with the minimum level of intervention. It allows doctors to get a good idea of what they are up against before beginning treatment. As it is essential to every other department, if the Radiology department is not functioning smoothly, there is a domino effect throughout the rest of the hospital, affecting patient care and recovery, as well as discharge times.

In spite of its importance, there is no set pattern or policy governing Radiology departments in Irish hospitals. Often they are a law unto themselves, which is not always in the best interests of patients. The result is a massively inconsistent service, with the only consistency being the universal lack of resources invested in Radiology by the HSE. In every department there is a debilitating lack of equipment and staff, and the consequences are felt at every level of patient care.

Take, for example, the case of MRI (magnetic resonance imaging) machines, which are among the latest innovations in scanning technology. They provide detailed information that is of immeasurable assistance to doctors in making the most accurate diagnosis and deciding the optimal course of treatment. In all First World countries, MRI scans are increasingly becoming routine requirements for the application of best medical practice. In Ireland, some of the capital's major hospitals are operating without a MRI scanner.

Is there an impact on patient care? Yes, there most certainly is. First off, medical teams at hospitals with no scanner may be slower to order a scan from another hospital when they know a bureaucratic nightmare will ensue. Junior doctors, and even senior registrars, are often forbidden from making such clinical decisions because of the cost of outsourcing. Even the process of ordering the scan can take an entire day. So even before the machine has even been switched on, the scan is delayed. Once the order number has been procured, the medical team must write a letter to the radiologist of a hospital possessing this much-sought-after machine, outlining the clinical details and the reason for requesting the scan, with the order number attached. The MRI hospital will then book in the patient for the scan at a date convenient to them in between their own patient population. Depending on how busy they are, that scan date can be anywhere from a few days to over two weeks. In many cases the patient in question has to wait in hospital, in their bed, until the appointed day.

When that day finally comes around, an ambulance and nurse escort must be arranged to accompany the patient to the other hospital; sometimes patients are sent in taxis. This means that the ward the patient has left is down one nurse, making the jobs of the remaining nurses more difficult and reducing the care and time they can offer to their own patients. In the event that a ward cannot spare a nurse, agency nurses are hired at expensive locum rates.

Finally, there's the wait after the scan has been performed. This is almost always longer than a scan from one's own hospital, and usually has to be chased up with repeated phone calls. This further delays the treatment and management of the patient.

The cumulative cost to the hospital of not having a MRI scanner is therefore extremely high and represents a clear example of HSE bureaucracy at its worst. Besides the inflated price that must be paid for the scan itself, there are numerous extras, such as the cost of the ambulance, not to mention the cost of keeping a patient in the hospital for several days longer than necessary, or the time cost to an already overworked medical team that has to jump through twenty hoops in order to organise and follow up the scan. Then there is the intangible and immeasurable cost to the patient of having to wait, and wait, and wait and to be told day after day that there is no date for the scan yet. Once they have been scanned, the patient must then wait, and wait, and wait for the results, all the while worrying about the outcome.

Compare this to the situation where a scanner is on hand in your local hospital. In this case a request card goes down to the Radiology department. The patient is booked in for the scan within days, depending on how busy the department is. A porter takes the patient down a few minutes before the scan and returns him/her to the ward. The medical team can obtain a verbal report later that day, or the next day at the latest.

As MRI scans become an increasingly necessary tool for the modern clinician, hospitals end up spending cumulatively more in one to two years on scan fees alone than the cost of an MRI scanner. It is frustrating, it is illogical and it is not best practice.

FOOD AND FASTING

Anyone who has had to wait for a scan knows the hurdles and hoops they have to jump through first. One of these is the mandatory fast. The stomach needs to be empty prior to most scans, so patients are required to fast from the night before. This is a sensible precaution and is necessary to ensure reliable and accurate imaging. Problems begin to arise when there is a lack of definition and consistency.

'Keep him fasting, just in case.' That instruction was uttered by a medical consultant on an early morning post-take ward round. It seemed unlikely that the scan would be done on that day, but nonetheless the patient was ordered to have no food or fluids in the hope that there might be a cancellation. *In the hope* – such is the demand on our Radiology departments. There should be an onus on Radiology departments to inform medical teams of the scheduled times of scans as soon as requests are made. If that were the case, then medical teams would not have to keep patients fasting throughout the day only for it to prove pointless when the planned scan doesn't materialise.

More questionable still is the regular practice of keeping patients fasting for scans for which fasting is not necessary. Patients awaiting bladder ultra-sounds, for example, should not be required to fast, yet the protocol of 'scan equals fast' is often followed slavishly.

A typical scenario that illustrates the lack of clear policy or protocol within Radiology departments involves patients who are admitted to hospital during the night. In most Radiology departments, only x-rays are available out of hours, with exceptions for other types of scans only in rare emergencies. However, such situations often require a consultant to speak to the radiologist on call and personally request the scan. This allows the patient to be seen in the morning by the team that put in the request for the CT or MRI scan, assuming the facility is available at the hospital.

When the patient is first admitted, nothing is certain, but the medical team needs to keep the patient fasting for the scan that will hopefully happen later in the day. The scan request is sent down to Radiology, and hours pass. The patient waits patiently, and hours pass. He asks the nurse when the scan is going to happen. The nurse rings the Radiology department, and the radiologist tells her that the patient hasn't been booked in yet, but that she should contact the medical team in charge of the patient.

The problem here is a lack of consistency and coherent procedure. Some Radiology departments require written request cards to be dropped down for all scans. The doctors request the scan, Radiology reviews the request and decides in which order to carry out the scans. Scans not scheduled for that day are left in the basket for the next day, with no definite date appended to them. Urgent scans must be discussed on a consultant-to-consultant basis only. In other hospitals, all scans require junior doctors to come down and discuss them with the radiology consultant on-call.

So the patient is not yet booked in for a scan, and the next day's bookings are up in the air. The medical team has requested the scan, but has no control over when it will be done. The patient is left on nil by mouth, often for the entire day, in the hope that the Radiology department will fit him in. The end of the day comes, and there is still no word on the scan. At that point it becomes the intern's job to apologise to the patient for the poor quality of service and tell him he must fast again the next day, still with no guarantee of getting the scan done.

In emergencies, the consultant in charge will call down himself and request the scan, which means it will probably be done that same day. These emergencies are the rare exceptions, however. In the main, most scans are not that urgent, even though they are necessary. For non-emergency cases, this is the depressing reality: hooked up to intravenous fluids to avoid becoming dehydrated, waiting interminably.

I have personally seen patients wait for two to three consecutive days, fasting. It is only when they reach breaking point and kick up a fuss that things get moved along. This is an appalling and unacceptable level of service, not to mention unethical. There is no justification for it. A simple solution would be to require Radiology departments to give an appointment within an hour of receiving a request. This way the medical team, ward staff and patient would know exactly where they stand. There is no reason why this is not possible. It is a simple case of organisation and booking patients in through either a computerised or written system. Why this is not already the case in major Irish hospitals is incomprehensible.

THE OBSTACLE OF BUREAUCRACY

It can sometimes seem as if Radiology departments come up with certain rules just to add further layers of bureaucracy. Patients' records are a good example: when requesting a scan, the medical team is responsible for submitting with the request all the previous scans of the patient. This is not a bad idea *per se* in that it facilitates the radiologist in contrasting and comparing with previous scans. Unfortunately, the implementation of this policy often borders on the extreme. Situations arise where important scan requests get held up because the team cannot locate an old scan that is irrelevant to the current condition.

The search for the old films usually begins with scouring the wards and the patient's bedside. If you have no luck there, then you have to go and backtrack the patient's entire stay in hospital, to each ward they have been to and right back to A&E. The search inevitably ends in Radiology, where the intern must go through the scan store, reception and every nook and cranny he can think of. Is it a fruitful search?

Take, for example, a patient who has come in with a problem of the gastrointestinal tract and requires an abdominal CT. The scan is delayed because an x-ray of his leg from two years ago cannot be found. It is irrelevant to the case in hand, but it is deemed necessary for the scan request. Add to this conundrum the fact that it is the medical team's responsibility to find the missing films, regardless of whether they have been working in the hospital for a year or a day.

Ironically, the missing scans are often hiding somewhere in the bowels of the Radiology department. The result? Fully qualified and trained doctors spending hours each day searching for old, often irrelevant, films inside the Radiology department so that the request to scan their patient will be accepted.

It would make far more sense if Radiology kept track of all films and instigated an easy-retrieval archiving system. Medical doctors should not be blackmailed or put under duress to do Radiology's work in exchange for the 'favour' of performing necessary scans. It is their medical, ethical and indeed legal responsibility to perform requested scans that are clinically indicated. Furthermore, it should be incumbent upon them to expedite this process, not to raise ridiculous objections that add unnecessary hoops for doctors to jump through. The collective energy of the medical team and the Radiology department should be focused on facilitating and assisting the speedy and efficient diagnosis and treatment of patients. As it stands at present, most junior doctors would agree that the *modus operandi* of Radiology is more concerned with an appearance of power. They are in charge, and they want you to know it. It's as if they are doing their medical colleagues a personal favour each time they agree to expedite a necessary scan. The fact that they are happy to ask other doctors to spend hours searching for old films in their department is a clear statement that their time is more important than their medical colleagues'.

Another serious issue facing junior doctors when dealing with radiologists is restrictions on communication. Medical emergencies happen at all times of the day and night, but many radiologists permit junior doctors to speak to them only at certain hours of the day, for example between 9.00am and 1.30pm. Outside of these hours, the tacit rule is that the request must come directly from the consultant.

Let me give a couple of examples from personal experience. On one occasion I went down to the Radiology department to request an ultrasound scan for a patient awaiting an operation. The scan was necessary for the operation. Unfortunately, by the time we decided that the operation was required, the 'window of opportunity' for talking to the radiologists had passed. I was not allowed to speak to the consultant and therefore could not make my case. Eventually my supervising consultant arrived and was annoyed that all was not ready for the operation to proceed. The radiologist could not refuse to speak to him; the scan was done. All this while the patient had been left waiting, not knowing, first, if and when the scan would happen and second, whether an operation was indeed necessary.

On another occasion, I was trying to organise a routine CT scan for a patient who had been admitted to the hospital on Friday. We were pretty sure the patient was fine, but we needed the scan before we could discharge him. This was the Friday of a bank holiday weekend. The scan was deemed 'not urgent' and, due to the risk of medical litigation, the patient was forced to stay in the hospital over the long weekend. It was a waste of the patient's time and the waste of a bed, on a weekend when every bed would be needed.

The underlying assumption at work in the Radiology department seems to be that, given the chance, junior doctors would request unnecessary scans willy-nilly, and this policy lessens the chances of this. In fact, the truth is that junior doctors are very conscious of avoiding unnecessary scans and would request an urgent scan only if they were absolutely convinced of its necessity (or if someone more senior, usually their consultant, has asked them to obtain a scan). A better, more unified approach is needed, based on inter-departmental trust and respect, so that everyone can do their job to the best of their ability.

OUTSOURCING RADIOLOGY

If the truth of the matter is that Radiology departments are overwhelmed and too busy to provide swift reports, then perhaps it is time to outsource some of the work. The storage and high-speed transfer of detailed medical imaging is now possible, allowing for a scan in one hospital to be reviewed by doctors around the world. This is a solution that has already been adopted by many hospitals in the USA, and the results have been nothing short of a complete success. In US hospitals, emergency department scan results are reported back within thirty minutes. The report is sent back by secure fax and the radiologist making the report is available to discuss the results by telephone with the doctor who requested the scan. Scans from Out-patients departments done on an elective, non-emergency basis are reported within twelve hours.

Compare this with Irish hospitals, where even in-patient scans are often not reported for several hours to days, and where elective procedures take at least several days to be reported. Isn't it a remarkable idea that we could send our x-rays and MRIs to India and have the result back quicker than we could by relying on our own radiologists?

There are, of course, concerns attached to out-sourcing of such work. The first concern that is immed-iately cited is quality of patient care. But we don't need to be pioneers in this field. By using companies already affiliated with leading US hospitals, we can ensure a high standard of care and reliability. After all, the risk of lawsuits is even greater in the USA than in Ireland, so these hospitals would not rely on such companies were they not 100 per cent convinced that it is safe to do so. There are many doctors living and working in India who trained in the USA, the UK and even in Ireland. If their skills and training can be put to good use to provide a more efficient twenty-four-hour service, then surely it is something we should take advantage of.

The other issue often raised in relation to outsourcing is cost. Would it be costly to outsource our radiology overseas? The answer, quite simply, is no. It is actually cheaper to outsource work to countries such as India.

The important thing to note is that this is a realistic, practical and immediately available solution already being utilised by medical institutions around the world. By outsourcing our radiology, we can treat our patients faster and better, free up hospital beds sooner and thereby ensure a quicker turnaround time for those waiting on trolleys in A&E.

Chapter 5

Dirt and Bugs

It was nearly 3.00pm on a busy day and I had been on the go since early morning. I hadn't had a chance to eat breakfast or lunch and was absolutely famished. This is not uncommon, nor is it the point of this story. Patients and their relatives often leave boxes of chocolates or flowers on the ward to thank the staff members who looked after them. For a busy junior doctor, these high-sugar snacks often serve as the main source of nourishment during a taxing day, despite their clear lack of nutritional value. On this day, I needed it. I spied an open box of chocolates behind the nurses' counter and made a beeline for it. One of the nurses working at the counter called to me. 'I wouldn't eat those if I were you,' she said.

'Why not?' I asked her.

She told me how, a few months back, for the sake of academic curiosity, a box of ward chocolates had been taken down to the lab and tested. The rather unpalatable findings were an assortment of unfriendly bacteria on their surface, including MRSA.

Around the same time as this occurred, the staff in the hospital were required to do a routine screen for colonisation by MRSA. This involved sending a nostril-swab to the lab. The exact findings were confidential and not for our eyes, but suffice to say that I was surprised to learn that several of my medical colleagues had been colonised by the deadly bacteria. I myself had escaped contamination. That meant I didn't have to undergo the prescribed cleaning regime: a week of anti-septic skin washes and nasal treatment, during which time contact with patients had to be minimal. Worrying findings indeed, but are they surprising?

THE CONCEPT OF HYGIENE

In 1847 a surgeon named Ignaz Semmelweis was teaching surgery, obstetrics and gynaecology at a Viennese hospital. He noticed a shocking rate of mortality among both surgical and obstetric patients: one out of every six mothers in the medical student-run obstetric section was dying during or after childbirth. Ironically, in the same institution mothers being looked after by midwifery students scored a mortality rate of only 2 per cent.

Doctor Semmelweis investigated the unusual discrepancy. His findings were interesting, if not revolutionary. While the midwifery students were very particular about hygiene, the student doctors were not. In fact, doctors were shuffling between living patients in the wards and dead patients in the morgue without any change of clothing and only an occasional wipe of their hands.

Semmelweis implemented a new protocol of washing hands with chlorinated lime. Not surprisingly, the mortality rates dropped considerably. Other doctors around the world also suggested hand-washing as an important tool, including Dr Thomas Watson from London and Dr Oliver Wendell Homes from the USA. However, it wasn't until the latter half of the eighteenth century that the existence of micro-organisms was discovered and hand-washing was made mandatory in most hospitals. Since then there have been constant and continuous improvements in the realm of medical hygiene, including the use of sterilised instruments for all procedures and an aseptic technique for all practitioners.

So why is hygiene still a problem now, in the twenty-first century? The key is human participation. We can have all the advances we want, but if our medical staff fail to comply with them, we have nothing. It is one of the most frustrating issues within the Irish health system because the cost of negligence is high, and yet the solutions are so simple.

THE HYGIENE AUDIT

The results of the first hygiene audit, published in November 2005, revealed a shocking lack of basic cleanliness in major Dublin hospitals, with many falling below even the most minimal in acceptable standards and others barely passing. In all, less than half the country's hospitals were on par with recognised standards. A second audit, conducted in the first half of 2006, showed significant improvement, which is encouraging, but much work remains to be done. Furthermore, the reasons for the 'improvement' might not be all they seem.

The principle behind the audit cycle is excellent. It is a matter of simple common sense. A standard is set for whatever field needs to be addressed. Correct practice is compared with the acceptable gold standard, or the best-known practice. Through this comparison, deficiencies are identified and solutions are suggested. These solutions are then incorporated into clinical practice. The audit cycle is thus complete and practice is again reviewed in comparison with acceptable standards. It is an excellent method to review and improve clinical practice generally. In theory.

In my own experience of of hygiene audits, however, theory and practice weren't exactly intimate bedfellows. The hospital had already had the first audit, and the inspectors were due to return for the follow-up inspection. Tip-offs prior to their arrival caused a massive buzz of activity in and around the hospital. Someone in the upper echelons of hospital management had been informed of the auditors' impending arrival, and had passed the word on through to every ward. Thus we knew hours beforehand that the inspectors were on their way for a 'surprise inspection', and the entire hospital was launched into a flurry of frantic activity. Clinical Nurse Managers went through their wards hastily, making sure everything was in tip-top shape. Interns received impromptu tutorials, inducted into the mysteries of the storage cupboards and the correct locations of equipment, supplies and posters. Doctors were even told of possible questions they might be asked, and how to answer them.

There are two incidents I remember quite vividly from around this time. The first was when I was in theatre. It was winter and I often wore a T-shirt under my scrubs for extra warmth. This was a direct violation of protocol, as we are not allowed to take any clothing worn outside into theatre. Violations of this rule are common. Doctors routinely walk around the hospital wards in their scrubs, the same ones they will be wearing in the theatre, which defeats entirely the purpose of having scrubs in the first place. Furthermore, non-surgical visitors to theatre often ignore the hygiene protocols because they are only 'popping into the room' and don't want to change in and out of scrubs. This means they enter theatre with 'outside' clothes on, plus jewellery. In my own case, I had been wearing a T-shirt under my scrubs for a couple of weeks and had never been questioned. Then word got around that the inspectors were due. The theatre nurse in charge immediately took me aside and asked me to remove the T-shirt. I obliged, of course. As it turned out, it was a false alarm. An hour later I had my T-shirt back on and no one minded at all.

The second incident happened on the day the second audit did take place. This time the tip-off was accurate and the inspectors did turn up. I was in the clinical room, cleaning up my clinical tray after a procedure, when a nurse interrupted me.

'You should be throwing that syringe into the sharps box and not the clinical waste,' she said.

I looked at her incredulously, then at the empty syringe. 'But there is no needle. It's just a piece of plastic. Why throw it into the sharps box?' I wasn't trying to be pedantic. Waste discarded in the sharps box costs the hospital a lot of money. And while no one can accuse nurses of not being clean, one fad I have noticed is the improper use of sharps boxes for discarding things that could go into the clinical waste or domestic waste bins. Considering that each sharps box is more than double the price to incinerate compared to a clinical waste bag, which in turn is double the price of domestic rubbish, this is an important distinction to make.

'Well, I don't know about that,' she replied. 'But the protocol says that syringes go in the sharps box.'

I was stubborn. 'I'm sure the protocol says that about syringes with needles and you're probably right about that. But I think it would be wasteful to throw this into the sharps box.'

'We can discuss that later,' she retorted. 'The inspectors will be around soon and we should just follow protocol.'

'I don't think this protocol makes sense. It seems inefficient.'

'Maybe you should tell the inspectors that.'

At this stage, a senior nurse intervened and pointed out that I was right, that protocol was on my side. Nonetheless, the incident underlined the culture of blind adherence to (in this case, perceived) protocol, for no other reason than fear of the audit. I saw both doctors and nurses being extraordinarily vigilant, executing their tasks in a way I'd never seen before and have not seen again since. Today was the audit, and today we would shine – literally. Tomorrow it would be back to the shortcuts. It dawned on me that the audit had turned into an exam. Its original purpose and premise had been twisted out of all proportion. It was no longer about improving and maintaining a good clinical practice; it was about scoring high marks on the day, about memorising useless facts and figures that would never be used again.

So the inspectors came, ticked their boxes, filled their forms and published their results, showing great improvements in hygiene. Our hospital went back to operating as it had always done prior to the inspection, and undoubtedly will continue to do so until the next audit comes around. From colleagues in many other hospitals, I've heard nothing to suggest that this is not common across the health system. One thing is clear: although the hygiene audits have succeeded in improving practical standards and increased the availability of tools essential for the maintenance of good hygiene, they have failed to change attitudes and cannot accurately inform the public about the true state of our hospitals. I do believe that the first hygiene audit, the results of which were published in November 2005, was done properly because hospitals did not have prior warning. The results were staggering: 48 per cent of hospitals showed a poor standard of hygiene; 43 per cent were fair; just 9 per cent showed a good standard of hygiene. Publication of these findings shocked the nation and forced HSE management to take action and implement protocols.

The second audit showed great improvement: 4 per cent scored a poor standard of hygiene; 36 per cent were fair; and a respectable 60 per cent showed a good standard of hygiene. But if hospitals knew in advance of the inspectors' arrival, then it is not a true audit. In my own opinion, there was a political necessity for this audit to find the results it did; the Irish public was not going to tolerate a poor second showing. It would be wrong to claim that no progress has been made because there has been a discernible improvement in the level of overall cleanliness in hospitals, but by the same token it would be wrong to think that these findings reflect a genuine level of improvement.

MRSA

The MRSA superbug is a good example of how we are still failing to achieve acceptable standards of hygiene across the board. Methicillin Resistant Staphylococcus Aureus is a deadly strain of bacteria. It is an evolved organism that is not only potentially lethal to its host but also largely immune to what remains the best weapon of modern medicine: antibiotics.

Since the invention of antibiotics, we have made few to none new discoveries to aid our treatments. It is true that we are far from the days of relying on penicillin and that we have discovered and developed many different types of antibiotic, as well as refined our delivery methods. But our ingenuity is frighteningly limited when compared to the evolutionary capabilities of Mother Nature.

The first shock was the discovery of bugs that were resistant to penicillin. We soon came up with newer antibiotics to defeat these creatures. The strongest of these antibiotics is a compound called Methicillin. Now, with the advent of MRSA and resistance to this compound, even our strongest antibiotics are only effective 40 per cent of the time if the bug manages to get into the bloodstream.

There has been much discussion about the MRSA superbug in Irish news media over the past few years. The mortality rates for a person whose bloodstream is infected with MRSA are well over 50 per cent, and in some instances as high as 67 per cent. It is a very sobering statistic.

The MRSA bug usually festers on people's hands and in noses, or on the skin elsewhere, waiting for its chance to get into the bloodstream. Among hospital patients the bug finds the ideal victim:

people whose natural defences are already weak or bypassed. The majority of patients in an acute hospital have an IV cannula inserted into their vein. Many patients have IV cannulas for days on end, even weeks, depending on their condition. These cannulas are ideal for bugs like MRSA to bypass the first lines of the body's defence and get directly into the bloodstream. Other such bypasses are common on hospital wards. Tracheostomies involve a small incision directly into the trachea, to allow patients with upper airway obstruction to breathe. Naso-gastric tubes are another example. They lead directly into patients' stomachs, although the strong acids secreted by the stomach are usually sufficient to protect it from colonisation.

One of the basic steps in preventing the spread of noscomial (hospital acquired) infections is hygiene protocol. An example of this is using an alcohol swab to clean the tip of intravenous cannula prior to each use and to wear gloves while using it. To date, out of the hundreds of doctors I have worked with, I have yet to see more than one or two perform one or both of these activities. Many doctors wear gloves while inserting the cannula into your vein, but how many of them wear them each time they touch the cannula? The sad truth is virtually none. This practice is common among junior doctors and consultants alike. In fact, one might find that a doctor connects an antibiotic to one patient's cannula after having changed the drip in another just moments before, without washing their hands or putting on gloves.

These kinds of omissions are something the hygiene audit cannot test. If people know they are being watched, they will put on the gloves. But what good is it for a hospital to score well and have all the equipment in place when no one bothers to use it? Once again, the protocols posted on the walls and drilled in lectures are useless if people don't put them into practice.

HAND-WASHING

Nowhere is the spread of germs and its grave results more obvious than in hospitals. Doctors have every reason to be vigilant about personal hygiene. Yet even among doctors who take great care to wash their hands and maintain good hygiene, there can be lapses. Take, for example, a typical ward round. The team of doctors carries a bundle of charts with them as they visit their rota of patients. This is much more efficient than returning to the nursing station after each patient to get the chart for the next patient. A doctor may wash his hands before seeing his patient, but if he then touches the chart, his hands have become contaminated.

It's easy to imagine. The doctor washes his

hands, approaches the patient, has a chat and asks a few questions. Then he looks in the chart for some information before examining the patient. Or perhaps he writes a note in the chart after talking to the patient. In the first instance he has been contaminated by the chart, in the second he has contaminated the chart: it's a vicious circle. These might seem like minor lapses, but they can allow a deadly bug to jump from one patient to another, possibly with severe consequences.

A common myth among doctors is that they need to wash their hands only before each patient. In theory, this sounds fine. If they wash their hands prior to examining each patient, they won't carry any infectious materials to the patient. So he washes his hands, sees the patient, then writes a note in that patient's chart. The chart is now contaminated. Later on another doctor comes along and takes a look at that chart. He isn't seeing a patient yet, so no need to wash his hands. Or so he thinks. He takes out another chart and touches it: cross-contamination. He decides the second chart belongs to a patient he needs to see and carries it with him to the patient's bedside. He stops to wash his hands. He is clean now. Then he picks up the chart again, lays it by the patient's bedside and proceeds to examine the patient. The medical staff are like handy trains that the bugs can jump on and hop off, allowing them to spread far quicker and more effectively than they otherwise could.

The next obvious question is: why aren't doctors washing their hands more often? One colleague said to me, 'I don't have time to wash my hands between every patient.'

This is a fairly common lament from doctors. Is it the doctors' fault that they don't make the time to perform this important task? Does their behaviour stem from a lack of education around the issues and ignorance of the consequences? Or is the immense pressure and exhaustion an understandable, albeit unjustifiable, excuse for taking shortcuts? It's a debatable point.

Of course, there is a group of doctors who don't need any of these excuses. They are the ones who simply do not wash their hands between patients. I know many doctors who will wash their hands 'when they can', or 'when they remember to'. Oftentimes you have a doctor in A&E attending to two or three patients at a time. Washing their hands in between, as they shuffle back and forth, is considered too inefficient to be worthwhile, so by the end of their shift each patient is probably colonised by the bugs of the others.

Some doctors will argue that they need to wash their hands only after dealing with patients known to have infections. This is counter-intuitive because the time to contain the infection is before it reaches the symptomatic stage. Waiting until then means that it has probably spread to numerous other patients. By that stage, even isolation is nothing more than an illusion of false safety.

On discussing these issues casually with colleagues, I have heard some startling tales and revelations about hand-washing. One of the most shocking was: 'I suffer more than patients from not washing my hands. I've often got a bout of diarrhoea after checking plantars.' The plantar is a reflex elicited on the sole of the foot. Usually it is done with the pointy end of a reflex hammer. Some doctors use their keys. Others use their thumb – only to proceed to another bedside to insert a needle into another patient's arm.

There is no doubt in my mind that most doctors know and understand proper hand-washing techniques. Posters and protocols on these can be found on every ward in most Irish hospitals, especially since the second audit. The HSE has also done a great job in providing the requisite equipment: wash-basins, liquid soap, soft paper towels and foot-pedal disposal bins are all readily available. Alcohol gel dispensers can be found at regular intervals. The problem is, many doctors simply fail to use them.

THE ISOLATED PATIENT

More dangerous still is the practice of hygiene around the isolated patient. These patients have usually contracted MRSA or other such dangerous infections. The infection may not have reached their bloodstream, so they may not be very ill, but the idea behind isolation is to prevent further contact until the colonisation has been eradicated. There are strict procedures and protocol to be followed every time one makes contact with isolated patients to minimise the chance of spread. This includes washing hands before and after, and the donning of gloves and an apron to shield one's clothing.

In practice, however, lapses occur. A consultant on a ward round may decide he is just going to 'step in the door' and have a 'quick chat' with the isolated patient, therefore the cumbersome hygiene 'formalities' need not be followed. It only takes a few seconds of contact for full contamination.

Worse still are those doctors, both consultants and juniors, who feel that the standard protocol in this regard is impractical and a waste of time. They therefore ignore it wilfully. These are the same doctors who are less likely to wash their hands regularly.

Unfortunately, statistics and surveys about hand-washing among doctors are about as useful as a canoe in an operating theatre. No doctor is going to admit to unhygienic practice and if they know they are being observed, they will do all the right things for the duration.

THE CLINICAL TRAY

The clinical tray is a key instrument of modern medicine. This small, white, plastic tray, or in some instances a blue kidney dish, can be found on practically every ward of every hospital in the country. They are used to carry anything from antibiotic drips and injections to IV cannula equipment. Doctors are notoriously dirty in their use of these trays. Countless times I have entered a clinical room and seen used, half-full trays lying around after someone has finished with them. The worst is when people leave discarded needles and other sharps in these trays, putting the lives of others at risk from possible contamination of HIV or hepatitis. Imagine paying such a heavy price for someone else's negligence?

Thankfully, this practice is very rare. Education and vigilance have instilled a level of awareness that at least means nearly all doctors discard their sharps appropriately in the sharps box. The availability of small, yellow sharp boxes, which can be attached to clinical trays, has also done a great deal for the problem. This vigilance doesn't extend to cleaning the trays themselves, however. Wrappers of instruments, empty vials of antibiotics, used alcohol swabs, etc., can all be found lying around. I would guess that at least half of doctors are guilty of this. It falls to the nurses to clean these trays. The presence of dirty trays on their ward reflects badly on them and it just wouldn't do for a matron or senior nurse to walk by and see such a mess in the clinical room. Right or wrong, they will get the blame, though I myself have never seen a nurse leave a dirty tray behind after having used it.

Lastly, there are the doctors who will discard everything they have used, including alcohol wipes, plastic covers, cotton buds and medication vials. But even these conscientious doctors will not take the effort to wipe the tray with alcohol wipes to disinfect it after use. Even on such 'clean' trays, it's usually possible to see dried droplets of blood from the last cannulation or arterial blood gas measurement.

It is with great reluctance that I admit I have yet to see any doctor disinfect a clinical tray with alcohol wipes after using it. Is this the highest standard of medical practice in Ireland? It would appear so, and it is just not good enough.

REASONS AND EXPLANATIONS

So, what is it with doctors? Why are we so careless and at times flagrantly nonchalant about an issue as important as hygiene? It would be easy to say that this is purely a problem of attitude. That all of the precautions described above are simple, practical things that any reasonable person should be able to do as a matter of common sense. And it would be easy to say that doctors are monsters without conscience, or merely uncouth. To say that, because it doesn't affect the doctors, they don't care about it. But the reality is far more complex than any of these arguments.

In the main, doctors signed up to this vocation because they believed in something, because they wanted to be of service to others and to humanity. Most doctors work hard and tirelessly. They give up nights of sleep and weekends of fun. Somewhere inside each doctor is a young, wide-eyed seventeen- or eighteen-year-old who once stood outside the grand gates of a medical college and stared ahead in awe. Had that someone, who had such dreams and aspirations, been told how they would feel seven or eight years down the line, they would probably have cried and turned away. Yes, most doctors are compassionate and caring individuals who often care more for the health and well-being of others than for themselves. So why is a seeming callousness and apathy, so at odds with this description, on display in our hospitals?

I cannot think of a more classic example to explain this than a recent incident involving a close friend. Let's call her Jane. This woman is a thoroughly decent person, the kind who always waits till the end of a buffet queue and happily takes whatever is left. It would be hard to find a person who has a more pleasant or caring personality. Everyone who has had the good fortune of making her acquaintance says the same about her.

The incident in question occurred on her third night on-call in the same week. She was busily admitting patients in A&E. One of the patients was an elderly lady suffering from a chronic condition, who had been brought to the hospital by her son. He cared for her and knew quite a lot about her condition. Jane was trying to perform an arterial blood gas measurement (ABG) on the patient. This can be a difficult procedure, and painful for the patient, especially for an elderly person in a fragile state. Unlike most blood tests, which use a vein, it involves inserting a needle directly into the artery.

An arterial blood test is sometimes needed to acquire certain information: the state of a patient's oxygenation, the acidic balance of the blood and the balance of important ions. ABG needles are usually thick and long. This, combined with the fact that arteries are much deeper, makes the procedure more difficult and painful.

Doctors will often ask friends and relatives of the patient to leave the cubicle or room while they perform procedures. There is nothing wrong with this as relatives can often become uncomfortable when their loved one is suffering, which can be an added distraction for the doctor already coping with a tense situation. Jane did not ask the woman's son to leave. She never does. She simply gives relatives the option, should they wish to exercise it. She tried to perform the ABG and failed to find the artery at the first attempt. This is fairly common, though Jane was used to hitting it first time. She withdrew the syringe and placed it in the tray and began feeling again for the point where the pulse was strongest. She tried again, and again failed to hit the artery. She made five attempts, becoming increasingly frustrated, and the patient was clearly in pain.

The patient's son interrupted her. 'Excuse me, but would you mind being a little more aseptic?'

Jane, who considers herself a perfectionist, was humiliated and angry. But the worst part of it was that she knew the son was 100 per cent right. She had repeatedly used the same needle, had not worn gloves nor washed her hands in between attempts. It was a pretty poor standard of hygiene, and she knew it.

Silently ashamed and beginning to feel defeated, Jane discarded the needle, went away, washed her hands, found another ABG set and returned to finish the procedure, which thankfully she managed to do this time. In Jane's case, as in that of many doctors, this lapse was clearly not a matter of apathy or callousness, or any lack of conscience. So what is it, then, that results in doctors being careless with medical hygiene?

A BRIEF COMPARISON

Nurses have a far better approach to hygiene than doctors. They always wash their hands and always wear gloves, no matter how small or quick the procedure. I have never seen a nurse go into an isolation room without observing the proper procedure and wearing protective clothing. Nor have I seen them leave behind a dirty clinical tray; all of the used plastics and coverings are discarded. So, too, is any clinical waste, being deposited in the appropriate yellow bags. Not so with doctors. When they do actually bother to throw away their waste, it usually just goes into the nearest bin. Needless to say, throwing clinical waste and blood products into the general waste disposal bin poses a severe public safety hazard. These materials should be incinerated, and the yellow bins are provided for that purpose.

Why do nurses practice good hygiene? It is a combination of factors. In general, nursing training seems to be far more robust on this issue. Nurses have a huge amount of respect for protocol. While this can be a hindrance on occasion, in the case of hygiene it works to full advantage. In short, nurses are better educated regarding hygiene. They understand the reasons behind the protocols and therefore follow them to the letter. They don't take short cuts.

Another strong factor, I believe, is the permanency of staff. Nurses are usually assigned to a particular ward. Though they may do occasional stints elsewhere, to cover staff shortages for instance, their primary duty is to a single ward. This permanency gives a feeling of belonging and pride. Nurses feel responsible for their ward. A ward in poor condition reflects badly on them. Not only that, as nurses work together all the time, if one isn't pulling their weight, then others obviously suffer. When that happens, the offender is quickly set right by her colleagues. It also means that if something goes wrong, a nurse cannot blame anyone else.

In direct contrast to this are doctors, who are not assigned to wards, but rather to consultants. This means they have a much-diminished sense of collective responsibility. Also, doctors work in six-month stints, while nurses remain in one hospital for years. For doctors, this fosters little sense of belonging. When a mistake is made, it's all too easy to blame someone else and disavow responsibility.

Oversight and supervision play a key role as well. Each ward has an experienced nurse in charge, the Clinical Nurse Manager (CNM). This tends to be someone who is not only experienced in areas of nursing but has also received excellent management training. These nurses dictate and organise the function of the nurses on the ward, as well as dealing with any problems.

The result of this is that slack behaviour is recognised quickly, reprimanded and corrected. They set an example for the rest of their staff to follow, which makes them key to the successful and efficient running of the ward.

Doctors have their own hierarchy. At the bottom are the interns, or junior house officers. Above them are usually one or more senior house officers, though in reality they are more equal than above. The registrar is really the field captain of the team. It's his/her job to pre-empt all problems and ensure the smooth running of the team. Consultants oversee all they survey and have the ultimate say in decision-making.

While there would appear to be plenty of room in this set-up for adequate supervision, the truth is that there is hardly any. Apart from team ward rounds, it is rare for more than one member of a team to be present on the ward at any given moment. Indeed, on surgical teams usually the entire team, except the intern, is usually busy in theatre. This means the actual level of supervision is pretty negligible. It is all too often left to the observant nurse to correct an errant doctor in issues of hygiene. This is neither appropriate nor ideal and creates unnecessary, yet understandable, friction among staff: it is not, and should not be, the job of nurses to make sure doctors clean up after themselves.

The other downside of this allocation is the pressure doctors are constantly under. Most wards are divided into six-bed units, with a pair of nurses assigned to each unit. That's about two nurses for between four and six patients; the exact numbers vary from hospital to hospital. In contrast, a medical intern may have anywhere from ten to forty patients to look after. This has profound implications. A nurse on a ward in a six-bed unit does not have other distractions. Those are her patients and she does not need to leave that area, except perhaps when she is covering another nurse on break. This means she can give adequate time to any task and make sure it is done properly. The intern, on the other hand, has perhaps twenty different patients, who are scattered around all corners of the hospital. The intern has a list of jobs to do, as decided by the medical team on the morning ward round. There is usually something for each patient, be it bloods, the organising of a scan, or talking to family members. On top of this, as the first port of call in the hospital, interns are constantly being paged as things crop up with their patients.

The critical aspect here is the issue of time. Though nurses are undoubtedly very busy and work very hard, they do have certain rights that are not afforded to doctors and that, ultimately, afford them the ability to practice safer medicine. To begin with, nurses work a thirty-nine-hour week. Typically, a nurse will work three thirteen-hour shifts and have the other four days of a week off. In contrast, an intern typically works anything from sixty to 100 hours a week.

It is true that medicine is a high-pressure job and those entering the profession are aware of this. Part of being a medical professional is learning to deal positively with this pressure. But everyone has a breaking-point. When doctors are grossly overworked, exhausted mentally and physically and under constant, unremitting pressure from all corners, that's when they begin to take short cuts and make excuses. Do they stop to wash their hands, or rush to the next patient? A recent study reveals that during a typical eight-hour shift, including an hour-long break, an ICU nurse should spend upwards of fifty minutes in hand-washing, if he is to do it properly. That is fifty minutes of hand-washing every seven-hour shift, which is a lot of time not spent on jobs people are urging you to do.

Adequate breaks is another key issue in this regard. Nurses have what we call 'protected breaks'. The length and frequency of their breaks depends on the duration of the shift, but typically they would have at least an hour for lunch and a couple of other, shorter breaks in between. Regardless of how busy it is, they will have time to take this break and the other nurses assigned to the ward will cover them. These time-outs are necessary for safe and ethical practice and should be upheld for all medical professionals. But they do not extend to doctors.

The other vital difference here is that, again regardless of how busy it is, a nurse will be able to leave the hospital at the end of the allotted shift. Contrast this to doctors: there is usually no one to cover them, so they can only take a break when there is no work pending, which in a hospital situation roughly translates as never. There are no allocated shifts. Though 'officially' they work 9.00am to 5.00pm, most surgical interns find themselves in work at 7.00am and, at best, don't get to leave until around the same time that evening. Within those twelve hours, they might have had fifteen minutes in total to grab a quick sandwich.

The picture that begins to emerge is one of a profession under siege. Most doctors who fail to wash their hands regularly don't do so out of apathy or callousness nor indeed a lack of education. They do it because they feel the constant pressure of time and the piling up of unfinished work. Under these circumstances, they end up taking short cuts. The first area to suffer will always be those without immediate consequences, and that means hygiene.

FIXING THE PROBLEMS

First, we need to facilitate staff and make it as easy as possible for them to maintain high standards of cleanliness. How do we do this? We improve and design facilities to the highest possible standard.

Each six-bed unit should be equipped with a sink, anti-septic washing-up liquid, hand towels, a bin in which to discard them and boxes of gloves. In addition to this, alcohol gel dispensers should be placed at regular intervals around all wards. (In clinical studies alcohol gel has been shown to be as effective as proper hand-washing and is much quicker.) These provisions are basic needs. People are unlikely to go searching for a place to wash their hands, or searching for gloves to wear when they are busy. It has to be made very easy for them.

There should be a box of small-, medium- and large-sized gloves next to each sink. Most of the time only one size can be found on the entire ward. For medical procedures that require the sensation of 'fine touch', it is vital that the correct size is available. I have often had to search around the ward for the correct size glove because I've made it my own protocol to always wear them while performing a procedure. When the proper gloves are not available, many doctors fall out of the habit of wearing them – in spite of the fact that in a needle-stick injury, a single layer of gloving will reduce the risk of infection by over 90 per cent – and end up in a pattern of unsafe medical practice.

The other thing that is rarely where it is supposed to be is the small, yellow sharps disposal box. In the clinical room these are generally either full or simply not to be found. Again, I've wasted much time looking all over the ward, eventually even checking the ward's store before giving up entirely. The end result is that a doctor is walking around with a contaminated needle in his tray or hand.

Then there are the clinical waste bins, yet another item that one can never find. No one is directly responsible to ensure that everything is in its place. Some say it is the job of the nurses on the ward, as they will be the first to know when anything is running short. Others say it is the duty of the hospital cleaning staff to ensure there is adequate supply. The lack of clearly defined roles is a great obstacle to efficient functioning.

These basic needs have to be met first and foremost. It's a very simple task to ensure adequate supply of these essential items. What good are the millions of euro supposedly pumped into the health service each year if doctors cannot find the proper sized gloves or a receptacle to dispose of hazardous materials?

Secondly, we need to improve education about hygiene and increase levels of awareness. It is assumed that doctors are taught this in medical school, but sadly, it is not in enough depth. Common sense and jurisprudence on their own aren't enough. I would say there would need to be at least three compulsory, one-hour sessions in every six-month rotation. Doctors need to be confronted about their myths of hygiene and current practices. They need to be exposed to and to discuss journal articles that prove the obvious benefits of good hygiene. Until doctors are themselves convinced of the need for routine hand-washing, wearing gloves and other basic precautions, improvement will be slow. Consultants must lead by example as aspiring juniors will often mirror those under whom they work initially. Old habits die hard, however, so it's important that consultants not become personally offended by suggestions to improve their practice.

After all, medicine is a constantly evolving profession. There is always room for betterment.

Next, we need to think of lateral solutions to the problem and find ways of getting people on board. There needs to be increased levels of supervision and indeed accountability. The working environment for doctors needs to be improved drastically. Doctors need to feel that they can give adequate time to their work and be able to do it properly, without having to take short cuts. This is obviously a complex issue, requiring widespread debate, discussion and consideration. Patients should be made aware what to expect, which in itself can serve as a tool for monitoring and improvement.

In conclusion, it is clear that our standards of hygiene are far below the standard we would like to achieve and that this is having a negative effect on patient care. It needs to be addressed immediately and comprehensively. The longer-term view requires continuing self-evaluation and education, and a system of robust auditing to bring us to standards that should be a comfortable minimum for a First World country.

Chapter 6

On-call:

A Personal Experience of Fatigue

My very first on-call was on a Sunday. Weekend calls are starkly different from weekday calls. They are much tougher for several reasons, which I will outline later. Having your first on-call on a Sunday is possibly the worst shift to start with, yet in my naivete I volunteered for it. As a group of new interns, we were told during our induction that our job would start on the weekend and that we would have to do the on-call on Saturday and Sunday. They didn't feel like forcing any one into it, thinking it would better if we volunteered. 'Might as well get it over with,' I thought to myself. At least I would be guaranteed to learn a lot. After all, how bad could it be?

I arrived at the hospital full of energy and enthusiasm at 8.45am on Sunday morning. My first stop was the switch, or telephone office. I proudly collected my bleep and attached it to my belt. It was now going to be mine for the rest of the year. It was a great feeling, knowing that people were depending on me and I had to deliver. I cherished the responsibility that came with the innocuous-looking black box.

I asked for the bleep number of the girl who had been on-call the previous day. An idealist like me, she had volunteered for the Saturday call. The debate about whether Saturday or Sunday is worse to be on-call is ongoing among interns. Each has its benefits and drawbacks. The advantage of a Saturday stint is that it's only twenty-four hours. You start on 9.00am on Saturday morning and finish on 9.00am on Sunday morning. So you at least get most of Sunday to rest and recover before the week ahead. The downside is that you don't really get a weekend if you are working on Saturday. You can't really go out Friday night because you need to be alert for work the next morning, and Sunday is spent mostly sleeping. You don't get any sort of a weekend break if you are on call on a Saturday.

Sunday, on the other hand, is a much more tiring call. You start at 9.00am on Sunday and finish at 5.00pm on Monday. That's thirty-six hours straight, possibly without sleep. It makes the week feel much longer because by Wednesday or Thursday, you don't have much energy left and you really need the next weekend desperately to rest up. Of course, the upside is that being on-call on Sunday means you can go out Friday night and enjoy yourself all day Saturday, thus starting your working week on Sunday feeling more refreshed. Which is worse? The jury is still out.

I contemplated none of these things at the time. I managed to contact my colleague, who told me she was on one of the wards doing the bloods for the morning. The hospital did not have a phlebotomist for the weekend, which means interns have to do the bloods. The agreement was that the intern on-call the day before would do the bloods in the morning before leaving, freeing up the incoming intern to get on with the work. This was the principle at any rate. In reality it depended on your luck – and how many bloods had been ordered.

I asked my colleague how the call had gone and, being the eternal optimist, she replied, 'Ah, it was grand, got about two hours of sleep.'

'God, you must be exhausted, was it really busy?'

'It was grand! Just a few things here and there.'

'You need to go home and get some rest, seriously.'

'Honestly, it's fine,' she replied. 'I'll just do these bloods.'

'No, no, it's okay. I'll do them. You go home and get some rest.'

Eventually I convinced her to go home. She handed me the cardiac arrest bleep. We each had our own bleeps that identified us uniquely. In addition to that, four doctors – one intern, two SHOs and a registrar – carried the special cardiac arrest bleep at all times. This was the emergency bleep that would go off within moments of a patient having an arrest anywhere in the hospital. When that bleep sounded, we were to instantly drop whatever we were doing and run to the location of the arrest.

So began my first day on-call. The first thing was to finish the morning bloods. Once I got that out of the way, I would be able to tackle the rest of my duties. Although a qualified doctor, like all my colleagues I had taken blood a total of three times prior to this, though I had practiced a few times on mannequins. Suffice to say that I was not brimming over with confidence in my abilities.

I headed down to the cardiology ward and introduced myself to the nurses there. They were very friendly and helpful. Some of them had many years of experience and were used to a new batch of green interns coming to wreak havoc on their wards every year. Only five patients on the ward needed to have blood taken that morning, and most of it was routine for the monitoring of serial data following heart attacks. A few of the patients also needed their IV cannulas replaced.

A nurse accompanied me into the clinical room and helped me gather the necessary ingredients: tourniquet, needles, alcohol swabs, a pair of gloves, bottles for the blood and some cotton. Thus armed, I made my way to the room. The patient was a fit and healthy-looking man in his mid-thirties. I was relieved to see bulging veins on his well-muscled arms.

I introduced myself and told the patient that he needed to have some bloods taken for routine tests, plus an IV cannula because the previous one had stopped working. He was very compliant and at ease.

'Go right ahead, Doctor, and do what you have to do.'

He put down his paper on the table beside the chair on which he was sitting. I went to the sink in the room and made a big show of washing my hands thoroughly. I dried them and donned the gloves. I asked him to straighten his arm and wrapped the tourniquet around his biceps. This I tightened considerably, probably too much in hindsight. I cleaned the area with an alcohol swab, knelt down on the ground beside him and unsheathed the needle, aiming it at the big, bulging vein in the centre of his arm.

Success! My first cannulation – I was overjoyed.

I pushed the plastic cannula into the vein and drew back the needle. The safety feature clicked in, covering the tip of the needle as it came out of the cannula and went into my clinical tray. In my excitement, though, I had left the tourniquet on and blood poured out of the open cannula, down the patient's arm and onto the floor in large spurts. Horrified, I quickly affixed the 'bung' to the end of the cannula and taped it down.

I apologised to the bemused patient and his family, cleaned up the blood with some tissues, and said a silent prayer of thanks that I had been wearing gloves, otherwise my hands would have been completely bloodied. Now the cannula, inserted, I had to take the blood. I informed the patient that I would need to use another needle. I did not know at the time that I could use the cannula I had just inserted into his arm, having been informed by the nurses that blood had to be taken separately. Instead, I searched out another bulging vein with the smaller phlebotomy needle.

I missed. Today, I could probably do it with my eyes closed, both hands tied behind my back and using my teeth. But on that first day, I missed. I apologised profusely again and removed the needle. A trickle of blood came out and I put a cotton bud on the puncture and taped it over.

The patient smiled tolerantly and told me it was

okay. I put the needle in the tray because I had no sharps disposal box, and removed a second one to try again. After a further three attempts, I finally managed to get it in. The patient was getting annoyed by this stage, but he was relieved that I had managed to find the vein.

'I'm really sorry about this,' I said for the umpteenth time.

'Ah no, you're fine, I'm just a bit worried about the colour of my arm.'

Indeed, his arm was starting to go bluish-purple. I had kept the tourniquet on his arm the entire time, preventing any circulation. He would not have any long-term problems, but would probably get some pins-and-needles once the blood returned.

I watched as the bottles filled slowly. I had four bottles to fill and each one was a juggling act. I was trying to hold the needle in place with one hand, attach the bottle to the end of the butterfly needle with the other and then pull on the suction to fill the bottle with my third hand. Off course, the lack of a third hand made this slightly difficult and quite comical. At least, it would have been comical had the patient not been thoroughly irritated by my incompetence. I didn't think of pre-suctioning the bottles – a simple insight that would have made the task much easier. I eventually managed to fill the bottles and hastily made my retreat. Off they went to the lab for analysis.

What a disaster, but at least it was over. The next job was more straightforward: just bloods, no cannula. Thankfully, I managed this on the second attempt. I grew in confidence with each successful attempt and sorted out the other three patients without too much trouble. I was interrupted several times by my bleeper. The other wards had jobs for me to do. While I was taking bloods down here, work was building up elsewhere. Nevertheless, I was beginning to feel more positive.

It was then that one of the nurses informed me that the laboratory had called. There was a problem with the sample from the first patient. I had labelled the bottles incorrectly. I would have to take the blood again. It was a truly depressing thought. The patient wasn't happy about my previous attempts and now I would have to go back and tell him what had happened. After everything, he would have to endure being tortured by me again because I was too stupid to label the sample correctly.

Luckily, the nurse in charge came to my rescue. She knew the patient fairly well and knew that the bloods weren't that urgent. 'We'll leave it for now,' she said. I breathed a huge sigh of relief. Before I could celebrate my escape, however, the cardiac arrest bleep went off. It began with a loud, sustained beeping, followed by a voice message through the speaker: 'Cardiac arrest on _____ward. I repeat, cardiac arrest on _____ ward.' The cycle repeated once more. My first thought was, 'Where the hell is that?' I thought back to my induction for the quickest way to get to the ward and began sprinting. Several visitors and relatives looked on with interest as I dashed past them in my white coat as if I was competing in the Olympic 100m dash.

I bounded up two flights of stairs and raced down the corridor until I arrived on the right ward. The location of the arrest was obvious: there was a flurry of activity around one of the six-bed units. I entered and was faced with an overwhelming scene.

On the bed in the corner was the patient. He was connected to every sort of tube and medical apparatus possible. Oxygen was being supplied through a mask with a large yellow bag attached to one end of it. The anaesthetist was squeezing the bag every few seconds to simulate a breath of air into the patient's lungs. Drips were hanging on one side of the bed, running freely into cannulas in his arm. One of the SHOs was trying to insert a second cannula on the other side. It can be hard enough to insert a cannula under the best of conditions, but in an arrest that difficulty is magnified tenfold. You are under immense pressure for time. You need to get the cannula in so that you can start giving the patient urgent medication, such as adrenaline. You also need to take bloods to get more information. When a patient's heart stops, the entire circulatory system starts to shut down. The veins collapse and can be impossible to find. On top of that, rapid chest compressions are causing the patient's body to move vigorously, making it even harder to hit the vein with the needle. It is under these conditions that your skills are truly tested. It is here that it counts.

The cardiac arrest trolley had arrived and the sticky pads were attached to his chest. Another doctor was doing chest compressions at a frantic pace. A temporary barrier had been erected for the sake of privacy because the curtain around the patient's bed wasn't sufficient to include all the people clustered around. The heart monitor on the cardiac arrest trolley showed a wayward zigzag rhythm. It was not the patient's own rhythm, but that of the chest compressions forcefully pumping his heart. The medical consultant on-call, who was running the arrest, spoke a single command.

'Stop.'

Everyone paused. The compressions stopped, as did the attempt to insert a second cannula. The faint rhythm on the monitor flattened out, no longer supported by the chest compressions. Silence descended.

'Is there a pulse?'

He checked for a carotid pulse in the neck. Other doctors felt on the wrists for the radial pulse, the groin for the femoral and the front aspect of the foot for the dorsalis. They waited five seconds. One by one they reported in: 'Nothing here.'

'Resume chest compressions.'

The silence was exploded by the medics working frantically again. I stood there, dumbfounded, standing meekly by the side of the bed, waiting for someone to tell me what they wanted me to do. They seemed to have everything covered for the moment. Luckily, the team on-call from the night before had been doing their post-take ward round. They had been on the ward when the arrest occurred and were first on the scene. The team on-call that day had arrived one by one shortly afterwards. I had been the last to arrive.

One of the medical registrars finally noticed me. 'We're probably okay here,' she said. 'So if you want to go and do whatever you were doing?'

I nodded silently and left the ward. In some ways I was disappointed – it was my first arrest and I hadn't gotten to help out. Sadly, there would be many more opportunities. On the other hand, I was relieved. I was afraid that they would ask me to do something and I wouldn't know what to do. That I would look like an idiot in front of my peers.

I learned later during the day that they had

managed to save the patient. Even though I had made no contribution, I still felt a small measure of pride, of being a part of the team.

It was now noon and I was starting to feel a faint rumble in my stomach. A quick break for toast or a cup of tea would have been nice, but there was no time for that. I went back to taking the bloods. After many attempts and a few angry patients, I managed to finish them, apart, that is, from the two or three patients I had been unable to get blood from, despite numerous attempts. I had to bleep the SHO on call, who I knew would probably be busy in casualty admitting patients. There were two on-call together and the one I spoke to was very nice and understanding. I guess she still remembered her first day of internship. 'Don't worry about it,' she told me, 'tell the nurses that I'll come down and do them when I get a chance.'

For the second time in the day I checked my watch. It was now 4.00pm. I couldn't believe that time had flown by so quickly. That is the one, and probably only, advantage of being in a job that is so demanding: you come to work in the morning and progress from one task to the next, and by the time you get a chance to take a breather and actually think about the day, many hours have already passed. At this stage, I decided to take a much-needed break. I had been on the go non-stop since 9.00am. I had to eat something or I would collapse. Scarily, there was still an awful lot of work to be done.

The staff cafeteria was closed, which meant I would not be able to get a proper lunch. Instead I went down to the small coffee shop that caters for visitors and relatives, where I bought a bag of popcorn, a pre-packaged chicken tikka sandwich and a small carton of milk. I wolfed these down over the next fifteen minutes, interrupted twice to answer my bleep. Then it was back to work.

Each ward had a long list of jobs waiting for me. Most were simple jobs, like writing up patients for fluids or pain relief. There was certainly a lot of paper-work. Finished medication charts had to be rewritten, a couple of patients had been discharged by the on-call team and needed their discharge papers and prescription. Most of the work was administrative. I found myself woefully under-prepared. The theory I had been taught in medical school wasn't going to make me efficient in such tasks.

Rarely was I asked to actually medically assess a patient. I was lucky because I was in a hospital that was well supported and had SHOs who were seeing the new acutely sick patients attending A&E, while I looked after the wards. It would have been physically impossible for me to do both. The hospital was simply too busy. In less busy hospitals, the intern is responsible for both. In some ways it's good to get that kind of exposure because you learn a lot. But it's not safe, especially for someone on the lower end of the learning curve.

One of the jobs I had to do was review a chest x-ray. The patient had had a naso-gastric (NG) tube inserted earlier. This is a tube that goes in through the nose, down into the back of the mouth, down the throat, into the food pipe and follows it all the way into the stomach. It is used to feed people with swallowing difficulties, usually after a stroke. Before the feed can start, an x-ray is need to ensure the tube is actually in the stomach and not in the lungs.

I went to the ward and looked at the chest x-ray. I was confused. I couldn't see the NG tube anywhere. I had seen such x-rays before as a medical student, and the NG tube was usually pretty obvious and easy to spot. I went down to the patient and looked at him. He didn't seem to have an NG tube, at least none that I could find. I looked around on the floor and around the bed to see if he had pulled it out. Nothing.

Baffled, I called the nurse who had asked me to review the x-ray. I explained the situation to him. At first he stared at me as if I had five heads. 'What do you mean he has no NG tube?' He checked the patient himself, eventually arriving at the same conclusion. We went back to the nursing station, where he pulled out the nursing notes.

'I don't understand what happened,' he told me. 'They said in the handover to get the chest x-ray reviewed for the NG tube.' He showed me the nursing notes and there it was written, clear as day. Maybe there had been some confusion. Maybe the team had wanted to insert an NG but hadn't gotten around to it. Such a plan would definitely have to be in the medical notes. I pulled out the patient's chart and flipped to the end. Again, nothing. There was no entry in the medical notes referring to an NG tube.

The nurse apologised to me. 'I don't know what happened, but they said it in the handover.' The nursing handover is a done at each change of shift, where the latest update is given along with pending tasks. It is a vital practice that ensures continuity of care.

For the chest x-ray review to end up on my to-do list meant someone had to have requested the x-ray from the Radiology department. Porters would have transported the patient to the department. The radiologists would have done the x-ray, printed it and sent it back with the patient to the ward. A nurse or nurses had handed this over to the next shift and asked that the on-call doctor be called down to review the x-ray. All of this happened with a chain of maybe ten people. Somehow, throughout the chain, no one had noticed that the purpose of doing the x-ray, the NG tube, didn't actually exist. I shuddered to think that our services had become so robotic.

It was almost midnight when next I stopped for a break. Finally, I was done. I had finished all the tasks on all the wards, including writing up at least ten people for night sedation after being told that they had requested it. It was my first day, who was I to argue? I just wanted to get the work done with minimum fuss so I could sit or lie down. I was hungry again, but it was too late to order a take-away. I found a vending machine and was able to get a packet of two cream crackers with a cube of cheese. It would have to do. I shoved these into the pocket of my white coat and began the walk towards the residence.

About halfway down the long corridor, my bleep went off. My heart sank. I answered from a phone hanging on the corridor wall.

'Sorry to disturb you, but one of our patients has just spiked a temperature of 38.'

'Oh, right, are they written up for paracetamol?' I asked.

'Yes, I think so. But do you want to do blood cultures?'

'I need to do blood cultures?'

'Yes, it's hospital policy. Every patient that spikes to 38 has to have it.'

Fair enough, I thought. That was the policy. So I

trudged back down the corridor and up four flights of stairs to the fourth floor; I was too impatient to wait for the elevator. I had never taken blood cultures before. There were no pre-suctioned bottles. I would have to extract 20mls of blood into a large syringe and then fill the blood culture bottles.

Predictably, I was unable to find the vein. After three failed attempts I gave up and guiltily bleeped the SHO on-call. I was hoping she hadn't gone to sleep. She hadn't. She was seeing a patient down in A&E. She told me she'd be up as soon as she could. Fifteen minutes later she arrived, true to her word. I watched as she got the needle in first time and extracted the necessary amount of blood. She left me with the syringe and headed back to A&E. I filled the bottles, labelled them, filled out the form and sent them to the lab.

I was still not finished. The other wards had spotted me and decided to ask me to do a few small jobs since I was already there. I did them and managed to make it to the residence this time. I ate my improvised dinner and went to the intern-on-call room to lie down. I placed my bleep, the cardiac arrest bleep and my mobile phone on the stand next to the single bed. I dumped my white coat on a chair and fell into the bed.

It felt uncomfortable and unfamiliar. I was

worried that in my tiredness, I would sleep through the bleep. It was now 1:30am. I probably lay awake for half-an-hour, wanting desperately to fall asleep. When I woke again, it was to the loud shrieking of the bleep. I was drenched in sweat, even though it wasn't a very warm night. Fumbling in the darkness, I found my mobile to check the time: 2.30 am. I checked the bleep and called the number of the ward.

'The patient is complaining of a headache and they are not written up for anything. Could you come down please and write them up for some paracetamol.'

'Sure,' I groaned, 'I'll be over in a minute.'

More small jobs. I did them and came back to my room. The time was now 3:15am. More time spent nervously awake, waiting for the bleep to go off any second, before eventually drifting off. This time it was the cardiac arrest bleep that roused me. The message was as loud and clear as before: 'Cardiac arrest in casualty in five minutes.' It was 4.00am and someone was being brought in by ambulance.

I had gone to sleep in my clothes, so I just threw on my shoes and sprinted to A&E. I wasn't the last to arrive this time; only the registrar on-call got there before me. The SHOs arrived shortly afterwards. We waited in nervous anticipation for the patient. The registrar got us organised, assigning us tasks. My job was to try and get an IV line on one side.

We saw the flashing blue lights of the ambulance from the window as it drove up to A&E. The patient was rushed in on a trolley by the ambulance crew. They pushed it next to the A&E trolley and applied the break. Three people on each side gripped the patient. 'One, two, three,' they counted in unison and transferred the patient swiftly onto the trolley.

We started. A couple of nurses cut open his shirt, an oxygen mask was applied along with the pads from the cardiac arrest trolley. One of the ambulance crew gave us a brief history: 'Forty-five-year-old male. Got up to go to the bathroom and collapsed clutching his chest. His wife called the ambulance. Non-smoker, no known past medical history.'

The patient had already been down for thirty minutes before he got to us.

I attached the torniquet around his arm and tried to get the needle in. I pierced the skin and was rewarded with the tell-tale flashback that indicated I was in the vein. I carefully extended the plastic cannula into the vein and withdrew the needle. But when I tried flushing the line with saline, it wouldn't go in. It must have dislodged somehow. I muttered a curse under my breath. Thankfully the

SHO had managed to get her line in on the other side. She took a syringe of blood and gave it to me before attaching fluids to the line.

I ran to the station and filled in the blood bottles to send them off to the lab. When I got back a couple of minutes later, the patient had already received the first shot of adrenaline. The registrar called for a pause to check the pulse. Still nothing. The nurse doing the chest compressions was starting to look tired. I offered to switch. He agreed. I took over, putting my hands in the right position and beginning the compressions. I watched the rhythm on the heart monitor; it was quite feeble. I increased the intensity and it picked up.

Within minutes my arms were burning. I regretted sorely all those times I had thought about working out but chosen not to. I kept going for about ten minutes before switching again. We continued the cycle of resuscitation for about half-an-hour.

'Okay, stop,' the registrar called out. 'He's had adrenaline and atropine multiple times and he's been down for an hour now. I think we should call it.'

She looked around the room at the rest of us. There was reluctant agreement.

'Time of death, 4.40am.' And just like that, we switched off.

I stood in disbelief for a while. I had never met

the patient before, but I still found it hard to come to terms with the fact that this man had died in front of me, despite all our best efforts. My trance was broken by the agonising scream of the man's wife as the registrar broke the news to her.

I went back to my room and crawled into bed. But I couldn't go back to sleep. I kept thinking of the arrest. At 6.00am my bleep went off again. More jobs to do, I didn't mind now though, the work would take my mind off things. By the time I finished those jobs it was time for a ward round with my team. We had a long day ahead and a busy clinic in the afternoon. I made my way to the doctor's office on our ward to get the charts and blood results ready for the round.

Once I'd gotten everything ready, I ran into the changing rooms outside theatre and grabbed a pair of scrubs. I hadn't thought of bringing a change of clothes, but I'd been wearing the current outfit for the last twenty-four hours. Wearing scrubs is a fairly common practice among on-call doctors. Often doctors on-call will wear them the day of the call as well as the day after. They are very comfortable and no one seems to mind. At this stage, even patients are used to seeing doctors in them.

I managed to get through the day. It's surprising, a person's energy reserves. I was still surviving on a diet of mostly chocolates. I think what keeps you going post-call is the fact that you don't have time to feel tired. There are always so many jobs pending that you just do one and move on to the next. But I was much slower in executing my tasks than I'd been the day before. I was also more forgetful and more clumsy, but I got through. The post-call lull only really hits in the afternoon, especially if you get some lunch. It's then that you feel the full effects. Your body just caves and says, 'No more!' At that point, even simply standing up requires a Herculean effort.

I didn't have lunch that day because we had a busy morning and were in clinic afterwards. The hours ticked by and we completed our busy clinic. At about 4.00 in the afternoon, things started to slow down. I was standing by the reception desk, waiting for something, when my registrar came up to me. 'How are you doing?' he asked.

'Pretty tired.'

'Do you want to head off?'

'Are you sure it's okay?'

'Yeah, we're almost done here anyway. We should be fine. Go home and get some rest.'

I jumped at the opportunity. 'Great, thanks! See you tomorrow.'

I took a taxi home that evening. There was no way I was going to stand around waiting for a bus. I must have slept twelve hours that night and I was still tired the next morning when I woke up. But I had gotten through my first on-call. I had coped and managed to do all the jobs required of me. I was thankful that I hadn't messed up any patients or caused any problems. I was sure the next call would go better.

Chapter 7

Working with Fatigue

How many hours at a stretch can a human being be expected to work without rest or food, whilst remaining effective at their job? How many hours in a week? At what point does a worker stop being effective? At what point are they in danger of making mistakes? Are current working practices in Ireland safe for doctors and their patients? Before I answer these questions, I would like to recount a tragic story.

I was in the canteen, on a rare lunch break with my friends, when we heard the devastating news that our colleague had been killed in a car crash on her way home from work. She had just completed a gruelling thirty-two-hour shift before the ill-fated journey. Throughout those thirty-two hours she had probably worked cheerfully and tirelessly. On-call at her hospital is notoriously busy and she was most likely on her feet constantly, being propelled by sheer adrenaline and lack of choice. In common with all doctors on-call, she was unlikely to have had more than an hour or two of sleep, if any, during this period, and probably little to eat. She was driving down the motorway, heading home to bed, when the crash occurred.

Although at HSE level nothing changed after this tragedy, policy was altered in the hospital where she had worked. Henceforth, any post-call doctor would be sent home in a taxi paid for by the hospital. It was a generous and thoughtful gesture, but it was also too little, too late.

What's most disturbing is that this measure isn't nationwide policy within the HSE. I guess it will take more such incidents before the HSE realises that there is a very real problem to be addressed. This is highly ironic: the entire principle of medical practice and good health advocates prevention rather than cure and yet here we are, stuck in a reactive rut. As long as the government thinks it is acceptable for a person to drive after thirty-two hours of demanding work, there will be accidents and deaths.

THE HOURS WE SHOULD WORK
In England, doctors work no more than fifty-six

hours a week, with a plan to reduce this to forty-eight hours in the near future. Their Irish counterparts are not so lucky, and yet the European Working Time Directive (EWTD) is quite specific on this detail, setting out the following deadlines:

June 2000: Timetable set to incorporate juniors into Directive.

August 2004: Interim 58-hour maximum working week. Rest and break requirements become law.

August 2007: Interim 56-hour maximum working week.

August 2009: Deadline for 48-hour maximum working week. This may be extended by another interim of 3 years at 52 hours, if exceptional circumstances apply.

The Directive is also clear in terms of requirements of rest and breaks:

EWTD rest requirements

The rest requirements, which come into effect in August 2004, are as follows:

- A minimum daily consecutive period of 11 hours

- A minimum rest break of 20 minutes when the working day exceeds 6 hours

- A minimum rest period of 24 hours in each
seven day period (this can be averaged to be a
48 hour rest period in 14 days)
- A minimum of four weeks' paid annual leave
- A maximum of eight hours' work in each 24
hours for night workers.

What has been the Irish government's response to
this? As has happened so often before, the government has shown its expertise at putting its hands in
its pockets, staring wistfully at the sky and whist-
ling innocently out of tune. There have been a few
pilot projects around the country, but these are
taking place only now, rather than seven years ago,
when they should have been instigated. In typical
fashion, the government has ignored the problem
and made the decision based on number-crunching
rather than on what is considered acceptable
standard. They are happy to pay a paltry fine to the
European Union rather than fix the problem. Why?
Because it's actually cheaper to pay the fine than to
hire adequate numbers of doctors to do the job
effectively and safely. So doctors continue to work
in slavelike conditions, and the Irish Medical
Organisation continues to be powerless, it would
seem, to do anything about it.

During the First World War, studies were carried
out on munitions workers who regularly worked

sixty hours per week. Reduction of their hours to between fifty and fifty-five showed a corresponding and significant increase in output. This increased further when ten-minute breaks were added. These findings have been confirmed time and time again by various studies since then, yet the Irish government needs a European Law to force it into action.

What is the excuse the government gives for its repeated inaction when pressed on the issue by doctors and the IMO? That medicine is a twenty-four-job and that doctors themselves are the greatest obstacle to the implementation of this Directive.

Yes, medical care has to be twenty-four hours a day, seven days a week, 365 days a year, but that applies equally to nurses. So where does the distinction between the two come in? Why is one group asked to work thirty-nine hours per week and the other over 100 hours? Nurses have proper shifts, protected breaks and holiday cover. When a doctor is away on holidays, there are no additional doctors asked to come in and cover his workload. The HSE simply saves money by letting three doctors do the work of four, or one doctor do the work of two for the duration, knowing they are powerless to complain. In rare parts of the country there are 'rotating NCHDs', doctors whose job is to cover those on leave so that their teams continue to function at full capacity. But rather than being the norm, this is a once-in-a-blue-moon exception.

Why this gross discrepancy? Maybe it's because the nursing union is more effective, because nurses are empowered to take action and protest injustice and will do so in sufficient numbers if the government tries to exploit them. The problem is, I have no explanation for the mysterious inner workings of the minds of the Department of Health, which somehow decided it was acceptable to create this inequity.

The recently aired 'Junior Doctors' programme on RTÉ goes some way to making the general public aware of the hours a doctor has to work. It is fairly common for junior doctors to work between sixty and ninety hours a week. I myself have on more than one occasion clocked in well over 100 hours in a week, including marathon fifty-six-hour shifts where I managed four to six hours' sleep in total through cat-naps. I will be the first one to stand up and say that I do not feel safe taking the responsibility for another human being's health, indeed life, during such shifts. But I have no choice.

How many decisions of State policy has the Minister for Health concluded after a thirty-six-hour shift without any rest? The same question goes out to hospital administration, management personal and on-call rota organisers, who pencil in the names for three or four on-call night shifts per week. I would venture that these gutless bureaucrats and politicians have never had to work such hours themselves. It's all too easy to write someone else's name on a sheet of paper and pin it up on a bulletin board, especially when you don't have to do any of the work or bear any of the responsibility when things go wrong. It is wrong, it is dangerous and it needs to stop.

THE CONSEQUENCES

It is a common myth that mistakes are not made, that any problems arising do so simply from the fact that doctors are fallible, like everyone else. Despite what is said by members of the profession, no doubt to protect against litigation, mistakes *are* made. Routinely. Most are minor and do not result in severe consequences; some do. Regardless, all mistakes are costly.

So what are the effects of sleep deprivation?

A study published in the *British Medical Journal* in June 2000 showed that after seventeen to nineteen hours without sleep, performance levels were equivalent to or worse than having a blood alcohol level of 0.05 per cent. A blood alcohol level of 0.05 per cent is considered hazardous in most countries. Furthermore, the study found that after a couple more hours without sleep, performance became equivalent to that of a person with a blood alcohol level of 0.1 per cent. In Ireland, the legal limit for drivers is a blood alcohol level of 0.08 per cent. This means that if you are being treated at 11.00pm by a doctor who has been working all day, you may as well be treated by a doctor who is under the influence of alcohol and unfit to drive. Yet this doctor may be expected to treat you for a further eighteen to twenty hours, before driving home.

For patients, the effect is two-pronged. The first is the direct effect on their day-to-day care. Have you ever had a doctor fail to insert an IV cannula into your arm? Was it because you had bad veins, or was it because the doctor could barely stay on his feet, much less find the vein and delicately guide a needle into it through the perpetual haze in front of his eyes? I've always considered myself quite adept at inserting IVs. Most of my patients have commented on how gentle I am. But I have noticed that when I'm post-call, I'm far more likely to take more than one attempt at cannulation or getting an ABG.

Another common mistake can be missing things while taking a history from a patient. Usually it's something minor that doesn't affect patients, but even small mistakes can increase a patient's hospital stay. This in itself is a major risk. The longer you are in a hospital, the more likely you are to catch a hospital-acquired infection, such as MRSA.

Missing or forgetting to request a particular investigation is probably the most common mistake tired doctors make. Again, these investigations are usually not urgent, but would probably need to be done at some stage, which might delay the patient's eventual discharge.

Nonetheless major mistakes, I would wager, are being made on a frequent basis.

I can give an example of this, involving another ex-colleague of mine. This woman is an excellent, very knowledgable doctor. She was called to see a patient who had become unconscious and unresponsive. This young man was being treated with insulin and dextrose for a dangerously high potassium level. She checked his latest results on the computer and found little wrong. She proceeded to perform investigations on the patient, including arterial blood gases, ECG and physical examination. She still couldn't pin down the cause of the problem and the patient remained unconscious.

She called her registrar for help. The registrar asked for the patient's blood sugar and the doctor quoted the result she'd looked up on the computer. It was only then that it hit her – the result was two hours' old.

While most blood results don't usually change so rapidly, blood sugars most certainly can. A finger-prick test can reveal the blood sugar in seconds. The most common cause of an unconscious state in a patient on insulin is their sugars being too high or too low. How could she have missed such a simple, straightforward and basic detail? Sure enough, when she did the finger-prick test, the blood sugar was dangerously low. The patient was suffering from severe hypoglycaemia. The registrar was not at all happy about this oversight. They treated the patient accordingly and he had to be transferred to ICU.

Thankfully for all concerned, this episode did not end in tragedy. The patient made a complete recovery and no permanent damage had been done. It was unusual for his blood sugars to drop so low, so quickly, but someone had given him too much insulin. The facts around that were never clearly established.

I remember this doctor telling me, with tears in her eyes, how ashamed she felt when the family thanked her profusely for saving their son's life, when she knew that her oversight could have left him permanently disabled. What if she had not been so fortunate and the patient had suffered permanent brain damage? Would an inquest have taken into account that she had been working for the last twenty-eight hours? I doubt it. She would have been stripped of her Medical Council registration and barred from practising medicine.

The Department of Health and the HSE take no

responsibility when doctors working under intolerable conditions make inevitable mistakes. It's always the patients and doctors who pay the price. Needle-stick injuries to doctors are the most common price to be paid, and most of these happen on-call. It happens time and time again: a tired doctor forgets to discard a needle properly during a procedure and pricks himself with it, or catches his own finger while searching for a place to make a second attempt. A momentary lapse of concentration is all it takes. These lapses are frequent at twenty-plus hours. And then it's over. You may have given yourself HIV or hepatitis – a life sentence.

Mistakes aren't the only transgression an over-tired doctor is likely to commit. A doctor awake for the last thirty-four hours is also more likely to deliberately take short cuts. This is when things like wearing gloves, washing hands or, sadly, even taking a shower get overlooked.

I believe that being over-worked is the main reason why doctors often don't practice good hygiene. As the effects are not immediately obvious, it's easy to dissociate oneself from responsibility. Was it your fault if one of your patients contracted MRSA? Lots of people were in contact with him; it could have been anyone. It's an easy get-out clause for an over-stressed, over-worked doctor.

The other unfortunate victim of the hours

doctors work is rapport. A tired doctor is less likely to take the time to explain things properly to a patient. People who are tired tend to get cranky and are easily flustered or irritated. On the other side, patients can also be understandably frustrated. They may have been lying on a trolley in A&E for the past eight hours. That would be enough to put even the nicest person in a foul temper. So you've got frustrated and annoyed patients coming to meet with exhausted and irritable doctors. It's certainly not the formula for the foundation of a beneficial doctor–patient relationship.

A study published in the *Journal of the American Medical Association* showed clearly that it is difficult to feel compassion for patients when fatigued. All these things lead to a serious decrease in the quality of service that we, as doctors, are offering. Undoubtedly, most doctors do their best to make an effort, even when extremely tired and under pressure, but there is a discernible deterioration that cannot be attributed to laziness or intent.

One study examining the relationship between long working hours and stress found that:

Long hours act both directly as a stressor, in increasing the demands on a person who attempts to maintain performance levels in the face of increasing fatigue, and indirectly by

145

increasing the time that a worker is exposed
to other sources of workplace stress.

According to the study, this stress affects doctors in terms of their behaviour, emotions and physical health. In terms of behaviour, we drink more alcohol, smoke more cigarettes and engage in more risk-taking behaviour. Emotionally, we become restless and fatigued. Anxiety and depression follow soon thereafter. Physical health also suffers, with an increase in blood pressure and an irregular or increased heart rate. Another British Household Panel study found 'high blood pressure, increased smoking and musculoskeletal problems with arms, legs, and hands to be direct consequences of moving from standard hours to a longer working week.'

The HSE needs to set out policies that will enable doctors to work more effectively, product-ively and to the greater benefit of patients. The policy on working hours for doctors in Ireland is the antithesis of this aspiration. Until it is add-ressed, it will be very hard indeed to secure other improvements and changes.

The other major issue that must be addressed with urgency is the fact that junior doctors are being thrown into the deep end without sufficient training. There are at least three hospitals in Ireland where surgical interns on-call are seeing A&E patients, with no A&E support doctors present in two of those hospitals after 5.00pm. This is diabolical.

Medical school provides a solid, but basic, foundation. This foundation needs to be built on considerably with practical training before doctors can handle emergency situations on their own. On their first day interns cannot be expected to do the same job as a SHO in the A&E, yet that is exactly what some hospitals in Ireland are asking them to do. This means that inexperienced doctors are handling surgical emergency situations without adequate support. The truth is that a day-one intern can barely manage to take blood and put in IV lines – having received very little practical training – let alone handle serious surgical emergencies. Young interns find themselves panicking when a surgical patient starts to bleed profusely. I doubt most have a clue how to deal with acute pancreatitis, for example. They may have the theoretical knowledge, but the practical experience needed before being thrust into the inferno is severely lacking. This baptism by fire of junior doctors is uncalled for and extremely dangerous.

Again, who takes responsibility when a doctor makes a mistake due to lack of adequate training? They didn't ask to be placed in that role. Just imagine the frustration of patients on 1 July each year – the day new internships begin. After a long wait in A&E, they find that the doctor coming to see them can barely hold the needle properly.

Despite this, there is a stark division among doctors on this question, with many strong advocates in favour of the status quo. The main reason for this is money: overtime pays well, particularly if you work a bank holiday Monday. For doctors from overseas, in particular, this is commonly very important as they are often the main earners in their family, with spouses and children to support as well as a mortgage. The basic pay of a junior doctor, which is around €30–€35k a year, doesn't go a long way towards doing this. As a result many doctors find themselves having to work eighty-hour weeks just to survive. They work their regular day job in the hospital, do on-calls on the rota, and on weekends and other free times they work as GP locums for extra cash.

The other argument cited in favour of long working hours is continuity of care. However, personally I think patients would opt for a fresh and alert doctor than the same one for a prolonged period of time, who by the end is little more than a relatively animated corpse. The UK has shorter working hours and regular hand-overs between doctors, with no adverse consequences reported.

The last objection to altering the working week is that it will have a negative effect on training: if doctors are doing only half the number of hours, then they will require double the time to train up to a high level. We must also look at the question of effectiveness in response: what can a doctor realistically take on board in a highly fatigued state? It would be overly simplistic to equate long hours with increased levels of knowledge and experience.

In Australia, junior doctors typically work no more than forty hours a week and there is absolutely no evidence to suggest that their training is inferior to their Irish counterparts. In fact, the Australian Medical Association argues that 'As fatigue depresses mood and decreases motivation, extended working hours reduce the effectiveness of learning on the job.'

It is high time that the Irish government stops dragging its feet and takes definite steps towards implementing the European Working Time Directive. Doctors deserve better, patients deserve better and it is up to us to send that message to our political representatives, loud and clear.

Chapter 8

The Failures of Geriatric Healthcare

The controversy that raged around the ill-treatment of elderly patients in nursing homes such as Lea's Cross is still fresh in the nation's minds. Fresher still is the fact that patients were wrongly made to pay for care in state nursing homes. Hopefully, by the time this book is published Mary Harney's compensation scheme will be in full swing and will go some way towards rectifying the error. From this storm of words, accusations and counter-accusations, one thing emerges clearly: we are very bad at caring for our elderly people.

I don't think this problem is entirely one of the HSE's making. It is in some respects a cultural problem, a moral one, and a reflection on the mores of our society today. One of the most heart-breaking scenes I have witnessed during my time as a doctor is the story of the 'Christmas granny', which perfectly illustrates how the new credo of self-absorption threatens the fundamental human links that are vital to sustain a sense of community, and humanity.

On Christmas Eve, my colleagues and I were hard at work in the hospital. An elderly lady was brought in to A&E by her relatives, who said she had a chest infection. The lady herself confirmed these symptoms. The A&E doctor had no choice but to admit her. Strangely, she exhibited no physical signs of an infection, her chest x-ray was extremely good for someone her age and she produced no sputum. The medical team hoped to discharge her the next morning, Christmas Day, so that she wouldn't have to spend the holiday in a ward bed.

When the time came to discharge her, however, they were astounded to realise that her family was nowhere to be found. It transpired that they had flown away for holidays, a break that had been scheduled for some time. The cynical reality of this sweet old lady's situation then dawned on us: not wanting to be burdened by her during their holidays, her family had left her in the hospital under the guise of a fake illness. The woman had gone along with this charade because she obviously did not want to alienate her family or get in the way of their fun.

Imagine that for a moment – abandoned at Christmas, feeling alone and unloved, while the people you love, you gave birth to and raised, consider you such a burden that they feel the need to unload you onto the health services for the biggest family day of the year. It was heart-rending.

If we could have taken solace in the isolated nature of this incident, it would have been some cold comfort. But it's not isolated. It's far from it. The 'Christmas granny' is a term that has been coined by hardened health professionals, who are fast getting used to the phenomenon because it happens every single year. Ireland, it seems, is wilfully discarding the family roots that once bound us together and made family and community the twin pillars of life. It is a deeper loss than perhaps people realise.

The dreadful and sorry truth is that abuse of the elderly is rife in this country. I was recently in the home of an elderly patient during a domiciliary visit. The house was absolutely filthy. From bathrooms to bedrooms, it was like something from a godforsaken shantytown in a war-torn country. How could the poor man's health not suffer in these conditions?

The man was unable to look after himself because of his deteriorating physical and mental health. His daughter and grown-up grand-daughter 'looked after him', and he paid them to do so. Despite the obvious neglect, I was powerless to intervene. The law provides little in the way of leverage to social and health professionals to protect elderly patients who, though not being abused directly, are clearly being taken advantage of in the most despicable manner.

I had an elderly patient who was not suffering from any illness. She had presented with an infection, which had been treated within a few days. Yet she was stuck in hospital for months, in an acute hospital bed, because an appropriate nursing-home bed could not be found. Her family flatly rejected that any such were available. The irony was that the lady had a teacher's pension, therefore could easily have afforded the comfort of a private nursing home. I was informed by the social worker on my team that this option was not available to her because her private funds were being spent supporting her daughter's illicit drug habit – the same daughter who insisted on keeping her in an acute hospital for months on end and placed obstacles in the path of any progress. Once again we were unable to do anything short of trying to persuade the woman that she needed to look after herself.

The problem of elderly people living in unfit conditions, with inappropriate care, or none at all, affects us all. The essence of medicine is prevention.

By providing clean, safe accommodation and adequate support, we can create an environment in which people need to come into hospital less often, thus vastly improving the situation for all concerned.

The critical shortage of beds in nursing homes means that elderly patients who are treated in hospital for minor medical problems can find themselves stuck there for months on end. Often it is the families that resist any attempts at discharge. They feel they simply cannot cope any longer and want the State to look after their relatives. But a hospital is not a nursing home. It is an acute facility with a high level of specialised care for people suffering with illness. Using hospital beds for patients who should be in nursing homes is extremely wasteful. We are in a constant state of crisis, with a shortage of beds, and yet perfectly healthy people are forced to stay in hospital because there is nowhere else for them to go.

A large part of the blame does lie with the HSE for not having enough beds to cope with the needs of our elderly population. But families need to take some responsibility, too. There are cases where people require high levels of care, which family members simply cannot provide. However, it is also the case that families are often unwilling to make the requisite lifestyle changes to look after their elderly parents. As a result, hospital stays can become protracted, with elderly patients increasingly at risk of contracting superbug infections. It is unsafe and it is unfair.

The process of finding a nursing-home bed should be initiated while the patient is in hospital, but they should be returned home while the placement is finalised rather than stay in an acute hospital. The nursing-home situation needs to be addressed immediately and improved dramatically. What is happening now is only the warning sign. As bad as things are, we are not at the zenith of the crisis. Currently, we have the luxury of a relatively young populace. However, those who ushered in the 'Celtic Tiger' are well into their middle age and it will not be long before the balance of our population shifts from being primarily young to being primarily elderly. That is when the demands on our health service will break the stretched elastic of our healthcare system.

It is important to act now, while the situation can still be salvaged. Failure at this crucial point will result in an unprecedented crisis in the Irish health system.

Chapter 9

Mental Health – A Neglected Service

In April 2005 a young mother turned up to a Wexford hospital seeking help. Sharon Grace was accompanied by her two children, four-year-old Mikahla and three-year-old Abby. She asked for a phone number for social services, but was informed the service was available from Monday to Friday only. She then asked for a phone number for emergency services, but did not receive it. Instead, the receptionist on duty offered to call Wexford General Hospital. Sharon Grace declined the offer, and left.

The following morning, her body was found, along with those of her two young children. Driven by despair and with nowhere to turn, spurned by a 'patient-oriented' system, she had gone into the river with her children and in it they had drowned.

Sharon Grace was known to have been a devoted mother, and we can surmise that her last thoughts were for her children. But they were failed, with brutal consequences, by a social service that turns off its conscience after 5.00pm.

Those three unnecessary deaths stand as a tragic black mark in the history of our health service. All the cheap talk of reform in its aftermath has brought about little long-term change. Indeed, at the inquest almost eighteen months later, it was revealed that the hospital where she had sought help still did not have a list of emergency numbers for social services.

The problems facing mental healthcare in Ireland are manifold. It is the neglected step-child of the health service. It is grossly under-funded, with a severe shortage of resources. Indeed, according to a 2007 report by the Comptroller and Auditor-General, only two out of thirty-six mental health districts are resourced adequately. Social services are inadequate throughout the country. Disparaging attitudes towards the mentally ill are to be found even amongst the ranks of healthcare professionals, and politics is rife.

Clearly, the system needs a radical rethink. Social services should be available around the clock, just as the emergency services are. Clear-cut criteria must be established as to what constitutes an emergency and what can wait for the next morning. It would be easy enough to execute and is certainly a necessary part of a long-term solution. In the case of the tragedy described above, if the system had been operating properly, options would have been created and a different outcome would probably have been the result.

How can we prevent such tragedies in the future? The key is accountability and fall-backs. The first step is to make it a requirement for all staff within the health service to establish a rapport with everyone who comes seeking help. The basic task of realising that someone needs help does not require medical training, just consideration. Once that need has been assessed, the appropriate service can be decided. In the Grace case, above, the psychiatrist on-call would have been contacted and informed that this woman was on the way. A nurse could then have escorted her from the hospital to a meeting with the psychiatrist, who would have been able to intervene positively. He would have assessed her state of mind and taken the appropriate action.

Most people who have survived a suicide attempt will tell you that they regret their actions and were not in a right-thinking state of mind when they made the decision to end their life. It is our duty to give them that chance, to give them a safe space in which to consider their actions in a clear and logical light. Sharon Grace wasn't given any chance, and she and her two children paid the ultimate price.

MEDICATIONS IN MENTAL HEALTH

Medication is an area of growing concern in the treatment of mental health in Ireland. We are developing a culture of cure by pill. There is a dire shortage of trained staff offering 'talking therapies', despite much research showing that therapies such as problem-solving, family therapy and cognitive behaviour therapy are highly useful in treating mental illness. Unfortunately, the waiting list for the people who 'cannot do without' such therapies is several months long, never mind the list for those who 'would probably benefit from'. The result is that we have an over-reliance on medications and there is a rush to put patients on some form of medication, whether or not it is appropriate.

There is a complex psychological game at play here. Putting a patient on medication often makes the doctor feel better. After all, as a doctor this is what you do – diagnose an illness and treat it with medication. It's familiar territory and easy to navigate. Most likely you will be able to find some justification to follow this path of least resistance. This ideology is supported by patients who, when spending €40–€50 to see a doctor, want more than just a chat. They want a pill for their ills and aren't satisfied customers until they get one. Often this results in poor prescribing practices, which are unhelpful and may even be harmful.

An example of such medication is Xanax, or Alprazolam. It is what is called a benzodiazepine and it is highly addictive. It also treats very little. It helps to allay the symptoms of severe anxiety, but has no impact on the underlying cause. Its effect is short-lived and the symptoms return within hours. Patients quickly become dependent on it, even when they have developed a tolerance that negates any beneficial effect. The word 'medication', in my opinion, is a poor description of this drug. What little therapeutic value it has is far outweighed, in most cases, by the addiction problems it brings. In fact, it is not available to be prescribed on the NHS.

There are some rare justifications for use of benzodiazepines, such as when a person is acutely unwell and at risk of harming themselves, or others. But even this prescription is justified for a short period of time only, numbering in days at the most; longer-term usage results in tolerance and addiction. The addiction to these medications can be as strong as an addiction to hard drugs. I have had patients who would do anything to get their hands on 'benzos'. To say that extreme caution should be exercised in their use is a gross understatement.

In spite of all this medical fact supporting a cautious use of these drugs, about half the patients visiting a mental health clinic in Ireland are on one benzodiazepine or another, and they are on them long term. Often it is their GP who initiates and renews the prescription, but psychiatrists are equally guilty. Once a patient has become addicted, it is very difficult to undo the pattern of demand and supply. Drugs such as Xanax make people feel good, they feel calm and able to cope, which means they want to take the pills. As a result, attempts to wean them off, for their own well-being, are strongly resisted.

Weaning patients off benzodiazepines is an arduous task. They become so addicted to the drug that they will do anything to stay on it, or to have the dose increased to deal with the increasing demands from their body as it gets used to the effects. They will exaggerate their symptoms and even invent new ones. Take them off it and their depression will worsen suddenly, without any precipitating factors. In the face of other work pressures and limited time, doctors often cave in and prescribe it for the stubborn patient, because it's the easy way out.

Often, psychiatric consultants who take the time to explain things to patients properly are branded as inefficient. This attitude needs to change. An improvement in prescribing practice will help not just patients but also doctors, who will see better long-term results of their work. But if we are to successfully introduce changes to prescribing practice, we first need to resource adequately for alternative therapies.

POLY-PHARMACY

Poly-pharmacy is the practice of having patients on numerous medications for the same condition. There are conditions and circumstances where this is justifiable, pain relief being one example. Patients suffering from severe pain often require more than one pain-killer to alleviate their symptoms, particularly post-surgery. Hypertension, or high blood pressure, is another example. For many patients a single anti-hypertensive is not sufficient to control their blood pressure. They might need multiple agents, with different sites of action, in order to keep the blood pressure limited to acceptable levels.

This tends not to be the case with mental illness, however. Most research suggests that for mental illness, less is more. Patients do not see cumulative benefits from additional medications, despite suffering the cumulative side-effects. Therefore, there is generally no advantage to having a patient on more than one anti-depressant or anti-psychotic.

Bi-polar illness is the exception to the rule because these patients may require a mood-stabiliser to keep them from getting high, but may also benefit from a mild anti-depressant to keep them from dipping too low. Generally speaking, though, the majority of patients should not be on more than a couple of medications for their mental illness.

Walk into any psychiatric ward or out-patient clinic in Ireland, however, and you will see a very different story written on the patients' medication charts. Many are on three to five medications, some as many as eight to ten, even though it's understood that if treating depression or schizophrenia with one agent fails to work, good practice is to switch the patient off that agent rather than simply add a second one. In today's world of evidence-based medical practice, the role of poly-pharmacy is mind-boggling.

The use of 'depots' in patients diagnosed with schizophrenia is another example of wayward prescribing. A depot is an injection given on a regular basis that replaces the need for daily oral medication. The contraceptive depot, for example, works for three months. In the case of anti-psychotic medication, the depot can be given bi-weekly or even monthly, depending on the medication and the dose. These drugs are used primarily when there are issues of compliance, i.e. when a mentally ill patient either cannot, or does not, want to take their medication.

Where, then, is the justification for having patients on both a depot and an oral medication? If a patient is responsible and reliable in taking medication orally, then why should they need the long-term injection? The patient should be on the right dose of the tablets to begin with. If they need an injection because they can't or won't take tablets, then why prescribe tablets? This sort of doubling-up is simply poor practice.

One area where the misuse of depots is glaringly obvious is in mental health hostels. These offer intermediate to long-term accommodation for mentally ill patients who are unable to live independently or with their families. There are trained nursing staff on duty at all times, who are responsible for the care of patients and the monitoring of their medication. Patients placed in these hostels are required to comply with their oral medication as part of a contract. Yet a glance at medication kardexes quickly reveals a different picture: patients being administered oral as well as depot anti-psychotics would appear to be the rule rather than the exception.

'PRN anti-psychotics should never be prescribed.'

This statement was made by a consultant psychiatrist during a teaching session for junior doctors. PRN prescribing is the prescribing of medication on an 'as needed' basis, whereby the doctor prescribes the medication but it is not a medication taken at regular intervals, but rather is taken by the patient, or administered by the nurse, only when there is a specific need for it. There are countless good reasons behind this consultant's advice. For example, anti-psychotic medications are routinely used as sedatives, despite their extreme side-effects, which can include weight-gain, generalised stiffness and, in the longer term, Parkinson's disease-type symptoms that can become irreversible. Patients taking these medications long-term end up needing other medication to counter their side-effects. Those medications bring with them their own set of problems and pitfalls.

The consultant's black-and-white advice to his juniors shows that while the knowledge is out there, out-dated prescribing practices are still rife in the health system. These need to be tackled and sorted out as soon as possible. Mentally ill patients may not be in a position to complain about their medication, nor have enough understanding of it to know when ineffective poly-pharmacy is being employed. That means it is all the more important for us to advocate on their behalf and to ensure that the treatment they are forced to take is appropriate and effective.

STIGMA

When a patient is ill, they normally enter what we call 'the sick role'. This is a period of time during which everyone understands that the person is unwell and is suffering. Employers and co-workers will cover for the unwell person at work and not complain that they are unable to perform duties as usual. The sick person gets sympathy from friends and family. In general, people are more patient and sympathetic towards the sick person. The understanding is that they are debilitated, through no fault of their own, and are the victim of unhappy circumstance. The hope is that the person will make a full and speedy recovery and be able to reclaim their place in society.

While in a sick role, the patient is expected to take it easy and concentrate on resting and recuperating. This follows on for a decent period of time after the illness has passed or been cured. The sick role is aided greatly by visible disability. When it is plainly obvious that someone is unwell – because they have a deathly pallor, or are using crutches, or are vomiting regularly – then those around respond accordingly and strive to help the afflicated person feel better. When you look sick, no one expects you to function at your normal levels, and you are given the time and space you need to recuperate fully.

In the case of mental illness, which is often

invisible, this support may be absent entirely. People who are depressed, for example, may not show any external signs of it to their co-workers, and often not even to their family. It is partly a vicious circle and partly the absence of a true 'sick role' for the mentally ill that lies at the root of so much social stigma surrounding these illnesses. The result is that the mentally ill often get categorised as having a problem with their personality, rather than an actual illness, as if the problem that has arisen were something entirely of their own concocting, and within their control to change.

This is not the case. Mental illness is just as much, if not more, debilitating than any other illness. Most of the time it is also completely outside the control of those who are suffering from it, even though willpower can be a valuable tool in tackling some of the elements. Mental illness often takes an insidious course. It can be very difficult to tell just what stage of illness someone is at, whether they are acutely unwell or in a chronic state, relapsing or recovering. The differences are often subtle and would not be obvious to an untrained eye. This is often a source of frustration to friends and families because one day their loved one seems to be getting better, then the next day are back to square one. Again, in contrast to other illnesses, mental illness can often have a protracted course, with many periods of 'two steps forward and one step back'. This unpredictability can be exasperating for those trying to care for the unstable individual. Families often lose patience when an assumed path of recovery is not followed. This, in turn, can have a profound impact on the mental state of the sufferer and add to the stigma attached to the condition.

In fact, this stigma can cling to the person long after the illness has been cured. Witness the practice in business of including a 'suffered from a mental illness' box for one-time sufferers to tick, regardless of how long it has been since their period of illness. There seems little regard for the fact that most people who suffer depression do recover fully and are more than capable of functioning optimally afterwards. The necessity to label oneself in this way suggests that mental illness is a lifelong condition.

The unhappy result of this shortsighted attitude is that people suffering from a mental illness often do not seek help because they do not want to be labelled for life. This means the stigma of mental illness not only affects patient treatment and recovery but also grossly delays patients presenting to the health service. Although steps have been taken by the HSE to increase public awareness of mental health issues, we must redouble our efforts in this field.

Sadly, the medical profession itself has no small

culpability when it comes to propagating this stigma. There is a culture within the profession that regards psychiatry as second-class, somehow vague and 'wishy-washy'. If doctors cannot lead by example and acknowledge the nature of mental illness, how can they expect the public to do so?

The crux of the problem is that doctors receive little to no training in psychiatry in this country. Most medical schools in Ireland have psychiatry as a subject during the clinical years, requiring students to attend four- to six-week clinical attachments. Students are influenced greatly by their seniors, however, and many hold a very negative view of psychiatry. As a result, the rotation in psychiatry is treated as more of a holiday than a clinical subject. Students invest the minimum required effort and attendance to pass the exam, and for most doctors this is the sum total of their exposure to and training in psychiatry. It is no surprise, then, that it occupies a second-class status in the medical hierarchy.

I have worked in the area of psychiatry myself, and I think it is unique in one respect: it is impossible to comprehend the true nature of the field without practical experience, without working as a psychiatrist and dealing with patients who present first-hand and without observing seniors deal with them. Admittedly, there is a very steep learning curve in psychiatry. I noticed a massive difference in my understanding and knowledge of the subject within a month of having begun working in the field.

I would be a strong advocate of compulsory training in psychiatry for all doctors who study and are qualified in Ireland. A year of internship is the current standard, during which doctors work for six months in medicine and six months in surgery. I would like to see this changed to five months in medicine, five months in surgery and two months in psychiatry. Even a brief period of two months would be enough to get past the initial learning curve and acquire a much better understanding of psychiatry, its associated illnesses and its benefits.

As part of their training General Practitioners are required to do a minimum of four to six months in psychiatry, and most will tell you that they benefited greatly from this experience. Those benefits are clearly reflected in the quality of their work. In my experience, the quality of referrals was much higher when coming from a GP than from a hospital doctor.

Better training and understanding of psychiatry in Ireland would benefit both doctors and patients greatly. It would help to reduce the stigma experienced by many patients. It would ease communication between general medical doctors and psychiatrists. It would smooth the way for patient referrals and the quality of the referrals would improve. A basic experience in psychiatry would also help doctors from feeling overwhelmed when faced with a mentally ill patient in the A&E. It is an important area, it is an area that deserves attention and it pays back dividends to those who take it seriously.

THE LOST BOYS

Young men with debilitating mental illness are an extremely vulnerable faction in Irish society. Sufferers of schizophrenia, for example, are often volatile and unpredictable. They require specialised care and careful monitoring. The illness may render them incapable of finding and holding down a steady job. Their families may be unequipped to cope and to give them the care they need. The end result is a group of men, often barely into adulthood, who are unable to fend for themselves, homeless, penniless and entirely reliant on a reluctant health service. Such men often find themselves admitted to acute psychiatric units for months, and indeed years, at a time.

From very early on, these men are taught to be dependent on the State and can easily become institutionalised as a result. How can we expect them to be rehabilitated and find some semblance of independence and normalcy without giving them a chance? What these men often need is a place in one of the country's psychiatric hostels. These are accommodations within the remit of the HSE that are used to house chronically ill patients. They offer numerous benefits over an acute unit.

First, psychiatric hostels offer stability. An acute unit has a high rate of turnover, with new patients constantly being admitted and others being discharged. Staff in these units cannot be expected to provide the level of rehabilitation care these men need while simultaneously dealing with acutely ill patients. The constant ebb and flow of bodies and emergencies also produces a significant destabilising effect on these psychiatric patients.

Secondly, while such patients are in an acute unit, all their needs are catered for in what is a highly controlled environment, as it needs to be. But it means there is very little drive or motivation for these patients to move out and re-engage with society. They are also deprived of peer-groups and find themselves very isolated in a crucial phase of their development as adults. Imagine an eighteen-year-old whose only contact with the outside world for eighteen months is visits from his family, or from other mentally ill patients.

A hostel, on the other hand, provides them with a safe and monitored environment. While they are living with other patients, the long-term patients tend to be fairly stable and not as intrusive as those in an acute phase. The hostel can serve as an important launch-pad because it allows patients to retain a great degree of independence throughout. They can come and go as they please, but are required to be present for medication times. This ensures compliance with medication, while at the same time permitting the freedom to stay in touch with the real world.

There are numerous inspiring success stories of young men who have been rehabilitated in this manner. Some have even gone on to hold down steady jobs, have relationships and lead a virtually normal life, apart from their continued need for medication. When this is the outcome, a huge burden is lifted from families and loved ones.

These beneficial effects notwithstanding, there still remains often strong resistance to placing these young men in hostels. There is no doubt that this group of patients requires a higher level of care and commitment, which can make their cases unattractive to hostel staff and management. Reluctance on their part to admit such patients means objections and obstacles are common. A nursing colleague described to me his shame at an incident he once witnessed, where the hostel in which he was working attempted to get an elderly lady, who was in alternative accommodation, moved back into their care in order to block the bed, so they wouldn't have to take in a young male schizophrenic patient.

In their defence, the hostels do make some valid points. The majority of residents in hostels are elderly. In many hostels, in fact, the average patient age is seventy years. These are patients for whom the traditional nursing homes don't have the expertise to manage their care. The argument is that this sort of environment is not the best place for a young man. If that is the case, rather than arguments we need more hostels designed specifically for young male patients. It is incumbent upon the HSE to provide the resources to meet the needs of all patients, including those from troubled backgrounds, or with a history of dangerous behaviour.

The Irish tax-payer is currently spending €350,000 per patient per year on each Irish patient residing in a private British institution, of which there are approximately a dozen. We simply do not have the appropriate facilities in Ireland to cater for these particular patients' needs. But surely at the annual cost of four such patients, i.e. €1.2 million, we could buy a house somewhere and staff it with trained health professionals? We could probably even do it a lot more economically.

I have attended countless case conferences concerning young men with mental illness, where the aim is to find the most appropriate accommodation for them. The result, inevitably, is a general declaration of why the patient is not appropriate for any of the available services, as opposed to a joint working solution to move things forward. Be it homeless aid, community nursing staff, hostel staff, families or long-stay wards, the familiar refrain of 'We just can't take him on, we haven't got the resources' can be heard resonating in the halls of conference rooms the length and breadth of the country. And so these patients, who already have enough in the way of stigma to deal with, also have to bear the burden of being disowned by the very health service professionals who are their only hope of salvation.

THE VICIOUS CIRCLE

There are many patients suffering from chronic schizophrenia, and other chronic mental disorders, who have their illness under control, are responsible with their medications and turn up for their out-patients' appointments, however they cannot hold down a job. A psychiatric hostel is not the best solution for these people. Out in the world, however, without a job, they cannot support themselves financially and are reliant on public services, which assists them in the form of the disability benefit.

They receive rent allowance, but it is capped at approximately €100 per week. If the rent is greater, the council will not pay a single cent towards it. Of course, the reality of the modern rental market is such that it is almost impossible to find suitable accommodation at such a price. As a last resort, many of these people enter a pact with landlords, who sign the official rent as being €400 per month, but in reality the patient is paying them upwards of €600 per month. This remainder of the rent has to be made up by the person himself, and comes out of his disability cheque. Once the rent has been subtracted, the patient is forced to survive on under €50 a week.

This is where it gets complicated. In order to make ends meet, many of these patients end up selling their prescription medication to local drug-dealers. This can lead to a vicious circle, whereby patients will go to great lengths to acquire further prescription medication, for example by feigning illness to their GP. So we now have already vulnerable patients selling their prescribed medication to drug-dealers, and leaving themselves short. Needless to say, it is not a situation that is conducive to continued well-being. Frequently, the end result is that there is a crisis episode of their illness, requiring repeated readmissions to hospital. If the rent allowance were realistic, these young men wouldn't be under pressure to enter this vicious circle in the first place.

On the positive side, the government is taking tentative steps towards addressing some of these issues. Rehabilitation Committees have been established throughout the country to facilitate the search for appropriate accommodation for those caught in perpetual limbo in the health service. What these committees will be able to achieve on the ground remains to be seen. The mere existence of the Committee isn't in itself going to magically fix house or rental prices, and it is not within their mandate to alter rent allowance for the mentally ill. Lastly, they will have to battle against the fact that facilities for certain types of patient, as described above, simply do not exist in this country. With all the good will in the world, the Rehabilitation Committees will find themselves facing the stark reality that they cannot house people at all, let alone house them adequately. Again, as with everything else in the health system, a multifaceted, interdepartmental approach to creating solutions is the only way forward.

THE ROT OF PATERNALISM

Discussing the poor quality of mental health services in Ireland, a consultant stated: 'There is a lack of respect, in general, towards patients. I don't see it changing any time soon.' He felt these attitudes were long-standing and pervasive, and that there was little will or impetus for change.

I believe there is a systemic attitude problem throughout our healthcare system towards patients suffering from mental illness. There is a lack of respect and consideration for these patients. Due to the nature of their illness, mental health patients often have their voice muted and are treated like children by medical staff. I have witnessed this attitude on many occasions. I have seen staff react dismissively towards their complaints; I have seen patients who suffer from complex and difficult-to-manage conditions get labelled as 'troublemakers'. One incident in particular sticks in my mind.

Day centres are the places where patients who are medium- to low-dependency spend the day. These centres are important institutions because they provide a safe and supervised environment. Patients attend anywhere from once a month to five days a week, as per their needs. The centres are run and supervised by trained psychiatric nursing staff.

During my work in psychiatry, I reviewed some of these patients on a weekly basis. The format of the review was as follows: usually the nurse in charge of the patient I was to see would sit down with me and give me some basic and very helpful background information. During this I would go over the patient's notes and medication kardex to gain an overall understanding of the case. The patient would then be asked to come in and I would take a brief history and make management changes as necessary. This is fairly standard procedure and quite effective.

One morning I was due to review a patient who was a long-term depression sufferer. The nurse told me that he was currently living with some relatives and that while he generally got on well with them, there were times of strife. She felt that it was during these times that he tended to get unwell. She said to me, 'Sometimes Mr A. doesn't feel like going to the hostel, but I think that he should still go, even if he doesn't think he needs to. Could you tell him that exactly?'

I was silently incensed. First of all, what was the point of me seeing and assessing the patient if I was being told exactly what my words should be? Secondly, the idea that the patient had the right to make his own decisions didn't seem to be anywhere in the picture.

The patient was called in and I took a history from him and observed his mental state. He seemed to be quite well and had been so for some time. He was also quite happy at home with his family and was managing excellently on his medication. There was nothing at all to suggest that he was in any way incapable of making his own decisions. However, keeping the well-meaning nurse's advice in mind, I mentioned that he might consider making use of the respite facilities available to him as he would probably benefit from regular visits. I felt that this kind of polite advice was within my remit and also reasonable. It wasn't enough for the nurse, however, who was sitting in with me. She cut in, in the middle of the conversation, when the patient was mid-sentence, to repeat her mantra: 'And, Mr A, we think you should go to the hostel for respite even when you feel you don't need it. Because you might not feel that you need it, even when you do.'

It seemed that the fact that this patient suffered from a very mild mental illness translated as a need for strict guidance.

On another occasion, I was asked to review a patient in a long-stay psychiatric ward. The consult, a request for psychiatric review by the medical team, explained that staff felt he was having a relapse of his illness. When I went to see the patient, however, the member of staff who had originally called me in was on his lunch-break. The nurse covering for him was surprised that I had been asked to see the patient because in his opinion the patient was not acting at all strangely or differently. In any case, I saw the patient and had a very pleasant chat with him. I could elicit no symptoms of a relapsing illness. I informed the nurse present of this and left the ward.

Later that day I received a phone call from the nurse who had initially contacted me. He wanted to know my opinion. I explained that I didn't think there was anything wrong and that the nurse present at the time didn't highlight any additional issues. I asked if there was anything specific about the patient that was worrying him.

He replied that the patient's family had been in contact and were unhappy because every time they talked to him on the telephone, he mentioned wanting to leave the long-stay ward and live with them. Indeed, he was under the delusion that perhaps they would come and take him to live with them.

I wasn't convinced that this was a delusion entirely. It was very possible that the family may have alluded to something or made certain promises to keep him calm. Regardless, this in itself was barely a sign of relapsing illness. I asked the nurse what he wanted me to do. Predictably, he wanted me to talk to the patient and tell him to stop annoying his family.

By this stage I'd had enough. I politely informed the nurse that I didn't feel it was our duty to tell patients what to say or not to say, nor how to behave. If he wanted to tell his family that he wanted to come home, then that was very much his right.

Really, does one have to be mentally ill to not want to spend the rest of one's life in a long-stay psychiatric ward? Is it not bad enough that stigma has robbed them of their independence and confined them, but that we come along and rob them of their dreams? Did it not seem the least bit paternalistic to this nurse to acquiesce to these requests? If the family wanted to not speak to him, or to tell him to stop asking them to take him home, then they could do their own dirty work. I would not be used as an instrument of oppression of this man's rightful freedoms. Luckily, the nurse agreed that it was a paternalistic attitude and so I did not have to enter into a deeper conflict to protect this man's autonomy.

These flagrant abuses of power are rife through-out the psychiatric and indeed general medical service. This attitude isn't limited to issues of auto-nomy, but often threatens the basic safety of medical practice. For example, I recently admitted a patient who was suffering from severe depression. He had been seen by the psychiatric unit and had to be kept in hospital, against his will, because he was in danger of attempting suicide. That evening, before I left for home, I was asked by a nurse to chart a sedative for the patient, 'just in case'.

This was perplexing. They wanted me to sedate someone who was already very slowed down? How was that supposed to help him? He would only be more likely to accidentally hurt himself on the ward in that state. But they wanted it 'just in case' he was upset later on. Of course he was going to be upset – he was being kept in hospital against his will. But unless he started behaving in an aggressive and threatening manner, there was absolutely no indication that sedation was necessary and, indeed, it might indeed have been a dangerous thing to do.

The nurses on the ward immediately joined forces against me. What if he turned aggressive and hurt someone – would I take responsibility then? It was utterly ridiculous. There had been no indication that he was aggressive and the nature of his illness was not one that would result in him becoming aggressive. This kind of blanket sedating of patients is a clear infringement of their rights, as well as being a highly unsafe medical practice.

Sadly, again I caved in to the pressure and constant badgering. Against my better judgment, I was pressured into prescribing a sedative for this patient when there was absolutely no indication. Later I spoke to my co-SHO about it. Apparently the same tack had been tried with her, but she had responded by saying, 'No, I don't think he needs it,' and refusing to argue thereafter. Perhaps I was wrong to allow myself to be coerced. Perhaps I was mistaken to try to explain my point of view from a reasonable stance. The nurses weren't interested in what was reasonable, they had decided that the patient should be sedated and that was all there was to it. I knew that had I also refused, the beleaguered on-call doctor would have been harassed until he gave in. That was one of the main reasons behind my capitulation on the matter.

Do the mentally ill not deserve their autonomy? Does the label 'mental illness' automatically strip a patient of his rights and dignity?

The last incident I will mention in this respect had perhaps the most far-reaching consequences of all. A schizophrenic patient was admitted under my team. He had suffered from diabetes for many years and due to his mental illness had very poor control of his blood sugars. While he was an in-patient under our care in the psychiatric hospital, we arranged an early appointment at the diabetic clinic because we could ensure that he would attend. He was reviewed at the clinic and we followed their recommendations. One of these was an increase in his insulin every two to three days until his blood sugars were at ideal levels.

On the last day of his stay, I was asked by a nurse to increase his insulin prescription once again. I reviewed his blood sugars and noticed that he had been down to a level of 4 just the day before, though in general they tended to be on the high side. I asked about the errant reading and was told that it was accurate, but that he had missed his breakfast that morning. Also, some of the recent readings were high because he was eating sweets in the morning and not complying with his dietary advice.

I decided it was unsafe to increase his insulin because his behaviour was unpredictable. Should he choose to skip breakfast at home, an increase in his insulin was almost guaranteed to put him into a hypoglycaemic state from which he might never recover. I politely explained this to the nurse. 'I don't think it's a very good idea to increase the insulin further. I think if his diet is so erratic, then a tight control of his sugars isn't really possible. We don't want to risk sending him into a hypo as he probably won't realise what's going on and present himself to the hospital on time.'

'But that's the protocol that the diabetic nurse recommended,' was the instant reply.

My explanation about the risk of increasing this man's insulin was brushed aside. All that mattered was the protocol. I tried explaining my reasoning from different angles, hoping to get her on side, trying to be polite and maintain a discussion rather than 'lay down the law.'

'We can't really regulate his insulin based on him taking a few extra sweets in the morning,' I explained.

She was still unconvinced. We let the discussion

hang uncomfortably in the air, not wanting to turn it into the unpleasant confrontation it was in danger of becoming. At this point the patient entered the office. After the usual greetings and outlining the plan for discharge, the nurse told him of the change to his insulin. 'We'll be increasing your insulin again before you go home today,' she said.

I was surprised. This had not been agreed. But the decision had already been made, it seemed. I left the office to perform other tasks, wanting to avoid an argument. So it remained the status quo until the time for the patient to be discharged was upon us and I was asked to write out his prescription. Once again, the insulin was brought up.

'So you're not going to increase the insulin?' she asked.

By now I had realised that I wasn't going to be able to persuade her as to the solid reasoning behind my decision, so didn't see the point of explaining it again.

'No, I don't think it's safe.'

'The diabetic nurse will be really unhappy. She said we should follow this protocol when we were over there.'

I decided to draw a line under the matter. 'Well, then she can find someone else to prescribe the insulin because I'm not going to,' I replied.

Yet again, the damned protocol. Don't get me

wrong, there was no problem with the protocol in itself, in fact it was an excellent protocol and would have worked well in most cases. But it couldn't take into account the individual circumstances and specific needs of this patient. I believe this kind of blind adherence to protocol stems from a medical culture that tells us: as long as you follow protocol, you are safe. In an increasingly litigious environment, the idea of taking individual responsibility is a thing of the past. As long as protocol is followed, it doesn't matter what happens to the poor patient. After all, when things go wrong, you can always stand up and proclaim loudly, 'But I was just following the prescribed protocol', thus disavowing yourself of all responsibility. It is a lazy method of medical practice and, more importantly, it is dangerous.

CONCLUDING THOUGHTS

I have outlined the main trouble spots within mental healthcare in Ireland: stigma stemming from lack of education and awareness; an under-resourced system with poor support from associated services; inadequate numbers of social workers and therapists to meet the needs of the population; widespread use of outmoded prescribing practices; lack of appropriate accommodation for long-term care patients; and, finally, undue pressure on junior doctors to prescribe sedatives or other inappropriate medications. On foot of this, what follows is a brief outline of the steps that could be taken to improve this situation.

1. Increased resources

Best practice guidelines recommend that each psychiatric team should comprise a psychiatric consultant, a specialist registrar, one or two junior doctors, at least one-and-a-half social workers, dedicated psychotherapists and two to three community mental health nurses, and that each team should be allocated a population of around 25,000 persons. According to the Comptroller and Auditor-General's report, only two out of thirty-six areas have full teams and many of these teams have to cope with a much higher than recommended level of population.

It is obvious that greater availability of accommodation for the mentally ill is needed urgently, along with more accommodation options. Long-stay wards and prolonged in-patient stays are not only bad for the patient but are also cost-ineffective. What is needed is an increase in the number of rapid response teams in the community. These are teams of trained staff who can identify a patient at risk of relapse and initiate early therapy, thus preventing the need for an acute admission and also serving to avert tragedy.

2. Increased education for members of the public, the government and all medical staff

The HSE launched a short-lived campaign after the Dunne family tragedy in April 2007, when the bodies of Adrian Dunne, his wife Ciara and their daughters, Leanne and Shania, aged five and three, were found in their home in Wexford. The local gardaí and the HSE had been aware of concerns for the family and the safety of the children, but the tragic outcome had not been prevented. Reactive campaigns are not enough. We need a continuous campaign, as well as open discussion and debate about the problems facing our mental health services and patients. We need to mandate training for all medical staff to ensure they have contact and at least a minimal amount of experience in mental health. This will help to change attitudes and foster a more positive environment for sufferers.

3. A review of prescribing and mental health protocols

A systematic review of the long-term medication of patients should be conducted. We need to ensure that evidence-based medicine is practised, not presumptive, 'just in case' medicine. No patient should be required to take ten different pills, especially not for extended periods of time. At the same time we also need to review how we choose to prescribe psychiatric medication, especially sedatives. A policy of 'less is more' needs to be understood, adopted and implemented.

4. More support for junior doctors, including twenty-four-hour on-site consultant cover via a shift system

In many psychiatric hospitals there is only a single junior doctor on-call. In my view, a consultant should be required to see every new admission within two hours of admission. This could be facilitated by implementing a twenty-four-hour shift system for consultants, on the condition that the system is resourced adequately. This measure is provided for, to some extent, in the new Mental Health Act, but thus far implementation thereof has been far from ideal. For all of these measures to work and to be workable, it requires a commitment to implementation and adherence that simply does not exist at present. But with education and a will to change, these badly needed revisions could become the norm in our hospitals.

Chapter 10

We are not racists, but . . .

Growing prosperity in Ireland has seen a steady influx of immigrants. We need this to keep our buoyant economy afloat. The health services are a prime example of this: without nurses and doctors from overseas, the system would cease to function. The truth is we simply do not have the systems in place to produce enough doctors and nurses to meet our needs. It is ironic, then, that medicine is one of the careers Irish people still emigrate to pursue, with many Irish doctors going to the UK or the USA for further training.

Despite our dependency on overseas carers, the attitude of the health service towards these employees is abominable. Studies by Dr Sam Evrington, a North London GP, showed that racism permeated every step of the career ladder in the NHS: European-sounding names had a better chance of getting an interview than Asian-sounding ones; top consultants were three times more likely to get a merit award if they were white; and black doctors were six times more likely to be disciplined by the General Medical Council. According to the British Medical Association (BMA), the NHS is intrinsically racist. It is surprising, then, that the BMA was ordered by a British court to pay over stg£800,000 to an Asian surgeon whom it refused to represent in a race discrimination case. The findings made it clear that the problems were not isolated and were indeed systemic. A 2002 Manchester tribunal ruled that the BMA was guilty of indirect race discrimination and that its conduct was 'high-handed throughout' and amounted to 'institutional denial'.

An article published in the *British Medical Journal* in 2004 concluded that the BMA was institutionally racist: a chilling indictment. But at least in the UK they are beginning to acknowledge and attempt to address these issues. Sadly, the story of the HSE and Irish health professionals has a different ending.

'If you want to progress your career, I suggest you leave this country.'
This was the advice offered by an Irish consultant

to one of his juniors, who was a non-national. Although he disagreed with the situation, the consultant recognised the practical reality for foreign doctors working in Ireland. He saw potential in his charge and did not want to see that talent stifled or discouraged by discrimination.

In my view – and I'm sure the consultant quoted above would concur – racism is widespread and firmly rooted in the health services. It is witnessed time and again when it comes to the issue of promotion: the non-white doctor will always find himself significantly disadvantaged. The bitter irony is that, even though non-national doctors keep the system afloat and help thousands of people every day, they are systematically overlooked when it comes to promotion and career advancement. The nature of hospital hierarchies means they are afforded little chance to challenge the inequity.

A young non-Irish doctor, who had graduated in Ireland, was working in a major Dublin hospital. He had applied for a specialist registrar training post when he was approached by one of the consultants for whom he worked. The consultant said to him, and I quote: 'I'm telling you this because I like you and you are a good doctor. But this job is going to be given to a white, Irish male. If you really want to advance your career, you need to go to the UK or the US.' Unsurprisingly, the doctor in question left Ireland for the UK a few months later.

If you want to be convinced that institutional discrimination exists, perform a head-count next time you visit a hospital. First, count the number of junior doctors you see. You will find that a fairly high percentage are non-white. Then, count the number of permanent (not locum) consultants. How many of them are non-white? This disparity will shock you. While you will find that over 50 per cent of junior doctors are non-white, you will be hard-pressed to find even one permanent, non-white consultant. This is because only 1 per cent of consultants working in Ireland are non-white. And still the HSE resolutely asserts that there is no discrimination. Does it seem like a fair and equitable process to you?

Non-white doctors are subject to the same career aspirations as white doctors, they receive the same training and the same qualifications from the same colleges. Their competence is tested and proven in the same manner. They are as good at or as bad at performing in interviews as their white counterparts. So why do they not progress in the same numbers?

In truth, applicants feel the sting from the very first stage of the process. I recently encountered a doctor who was fasting during the Muslim holy month of Ramadan. While this is a normal practise for those who follow the Islamic faith, I was perplexed because the doctor had a Christian name. I asked him about this, and he told me that he had officially converted to Christianity and changed his name so that he could use his Christian name in applications to hospitals. Apparently his countrymen already based in this country had advised him that this was the best way to get his foot in the door.

The next step, the interview process, is no better. In fact, it is an inside joke among non-national doctors working in Ireland that if there are fifteen candidates at a job interview for three posts and two of them are white, the remaining thirteen candidates are actually competing for one post. There is an unspoken hierarchy that decides which rung on the medical ladder you will be allowed to occupy. This is decided independent of experience, qualification or aptitude. On the top rung is the white male doctor who, provided he is competent, will get preference above every other applicant. White female doctors and non-white Irish doctors are next, followed by non-white EU citizens. Then we have the non-white, non-Irish, non-EU doctors who graduated in Ireland. On the bottom rung stand the immigrants, those doctors who have obtained their qualifications outside Ireland.

This is the harsh reality of the HSE, one that is disguised by a so-called structured interview process. Indeed, the interviews are designed to be impartial,

with candidates scored on the basis of their performance. The process is entirely subjective, however. If
one candidate scores higher or lower in the area of
communication skills, then how can he/she challenge
that? It is a purely subjective assessment by the panel,
but it has been given the veneer of objectivity to
support the illusion of equity.

TREATING PATIENTS IN A RACIST ENVIRONMENT

Racism affects everyone, including patients,
because it creates a power dynamic that disadvan-
tages the non-white doctor. Take, as an example,
the doctor who resides here on a working permit.
He needs his job to stay in the country, as well as to
support his family. Perhaps he cannot risk being
seen to not get along with other medical staff, or
challenging their supervising consultant when he
makes a simple mistake in patient management.
One bad reference can ruin everything, so he is in
an inequitable position and therefore vulnerable.
This gives rise to a power dynamic that affects how
this doctor will be treated by his colleagues,
possibly including nursing staff. I have spoken to
numerous overseas doctors who have admitted to
me that they find their patient-management
decisions challenged on a much more regular basis
than white doctors. And they do not speak up, for
fear of the consequences.

Doctor X

A CONSULTANT'S EXAMPLE

Dr Altaf Naqvi is a consultant surgeon working in Ennis, County Clare. He came to Ireland from Pakistan after completing his internship twenty-two years ago. He has only just earned a full-time consultant post. Dr Naqvi has long been highlighting the plight of migrant doctors, and in many ways he has paid the price for it. The fact that it took him twenty-two years to obtain a consultant post bears testimony to that price. For a white doctor, ten years is considered an average duration from graduation to consultancy. This includes one year of internship, two years as a SHO, two or three years as a registrar and then a further two to three years as a specialist registrar. Unfortunately, non-white doctors can spend decades as registrars without being able to advance any further.

Dr Naqvi has complained on several occasions that the colour of his skin has slowed the advancement of his career. He feels that, rather than being addressed, his complaints marked him out as a 'troublemaker', thus serving only to slow his progress even further. Based on his personal experiences, Dr Naqvi states unequivocally that racism within the Irish health service is institutional in nature. The distinct lack of non-white consultants in our hospitals would seem to back his claim.

Dr Naqvi also published a study on bullying in

the Irish health service. It shocked the medical community, but in typical fashion was dismissed by consultants, who pointed to the fact that hardly any formal complaints have been lodged. This kind of intentional dismissal of criticism is, unfortunately, the standard procedure for dealing with problems in the Irish health service.

One of the problems Dr Naqvi often laments is the lack of adequate training offered to non-white doctors. Presenting himself as an example he explains, 'One of my consultants said to me, "Don't go to theatre, see patients in clinic and do endoscopies. You are here for service work, what will you do with training? You don't need training because you are not going to become a consultant."' The racist arrogance of that statement is quite breathtaking, and shows just how much of an exclusive club the health service has become. Dr Naqvi is currently in the process of completing the first proper study on racism undertaken within the Irish health service. The fact that no such study has been conducted to date is significant in itself. An early compilation of his findings suggests that the rate of reported discrimination against overseas doctors via an anonymous survey may be as high as 80 per cent. The study is due to be completed and published in late 2007, when I expect the typical response from consultants will be to point out the obvious fact that overseas doctors cannot lodge formal complaints for fear of reprisal.

Most overseas doctors have learnt from Dr Naqvi's example and they do not want to spend two decades fighting in order to earn a consultant post that they deserve based on the merit of their dedication and hard work. The real danger here is that non-white doctors will give up. That they will decide to get on with their work quietly, ignoring the snubs, resigned to the knowledge that the system is corrupt beyond repair and no one cares about them or is willing to take their part. This would be the worst possible outcome because it would give free reign to the Irish health service, and beyond to Irish society, to indulge in discrimination without being challenged in any way whatsoever. As long as consultants are allowed to have full discretion over the futures of doctors working under them, our non-white doctors will be working in vain, as their efforts and dedication will never be recognised or rewarded. That sort of work would deaden anyone's soul, and destroy the vocation that brought them into the profession.

It is high time the Irish government and the Irish health service recognised the invaluable contribution made by non-white doctors and rewarded them appropriately. If the system treats people as little more than commodities, then that is what they risk becoming, with the attendant risk of a diminished and demoralised health service that fails to meet the needs and expectations of patients. That said, it is difficult to envisage a simple solution to a problem that is so systemic. How does one create a fairer job application and allocation process? Ultimately, it is not possible to do away with candidate interviews, which is one of the areas in which prejudices can gain a foothold over facts.

For my own part, I would propose a centralised system, whereby interviewers are selected randomly from a large pool of consultants from all specialities. These consultants should not know for which job they are interviewing candidates until just before the interview commences. This might help to eliminate the power of contacts, which drives the current job recruitment process. It would also loosen some of the stranglehold that consultants have over the health service. At base, though, the problem is one of social mores. In the twenty-first century, when migration is common and beneficial, the Irish people need to move towards a new ideology, one built on the tenets of equality and facilitation for all, not abuse and obstruction.

On a related topic, there is another form of discrimination that is rife in our hospitals, and that is the discrimination to which all candidates are subjected when they apply for a job. While it is true that the career ladder is far easier to climb for white doctors, it is still not a given that they will have an easy time of it. Regardless of the colour of your skin, the fact is that the current system of career progression is so inequitable that being on the right side of a consultant is ultimately more valuable than a clear ability to do one's job.

First of all, there is no standardised system within the HSE for hiring doctors. Individual hospitals operate as fiefdoms, hiring whomever they wish, as they wish. From what I have witnessed, questions of need, suitability and competence are often secondary in this equation. Consultants sift through the résumés of potential applicants and create a shortlist. The purpose of the shortlist isn't to ensure the best candidates are called for interview, but rather to fill the required number of interview spots to make the job seem competitive and open. In reality, it has often decided well in advance who will be awarded the position. Word-of-mouth, references and bolstering the ego of powerful consultants remains the best way to secure a good job.

The Dublin Area Hospitals Medical Rotational Training Scheme is one of the most centralised schemes in the country, whereby all the major Dublin hospitals combine together to jointly process applications and conduct interviews for posts of medical senior house officers. Over 1,000 doctors apply for this scheme annually, and roughly 200 candidates are interviewed for around 100 available posts. The process is supposed to be fair and impartial. Candidates are given marks based on their résumés, with extra marks for research, diplomas, degrees, memberships and academic laurels. The top 200 are subsequently invited for interviews, which are conducted by consultants from these hospitals. Again, candidates are marked at these interviews and the total marks decide who is hired and who is not.

Theoretically, in a fair and competitive process, this procedure should result in the hiring of the most capable doctors. In the end, however, the hospitals have a veto on all appointments, meaning they have the right to award jobs to candidates regardless of their score. Confidence in the system is largely eroded because of the existence of this power.

Recently, there was great concern among junior doctors as it was perceived that four out of the five of the major Dublin hospitals participating in the scheme chose to exercise their vetoes. It was a widely held view that certain candidates had been bumped ahead of those in the queue who had better marks. I personally knew several excellent doctors who were not even called for interviews, while other candidates with slighter résumés and accolades, but better connections, were interviewed and appointed.

Many of those who applied for positions, as well

as independent observers, believe this selection process is a sham, and will remain so as long as the final decisions are subject to such a veto, which is not justifiable.

The problem is that the entire system is opaque, and the participants have no idea throughout the process of exactly where they stand. There is no way for a candidate to see what marks they received in the initial written application. The system for awarding points is not disclosed. Candidates are either invited to interview stage or not, they are not privy to the scores which should be the determining factor. This leads to doubt and questions of partiality. If the system is fair, then why not make it transparent? As it stands, it's impossible for candidates to know if the system has judged them fairly, or not.

The next stage, the interview, is subject to the same lack of transparency: again the system of marking, and the marks themselves, are not made available to candidates. And, at the last stage of the process, as we've seen, hosptials retain a veto.

I have personally known people who have felt hard done by through this process – doctors at the top of the class, who are known to be skilled and diligent, with excellent communication skills, yet who somehow failed to get selected. I have known better doctors than me, with more qualifications than me, who did not even get called for interview.

In a system that is supposed to be objective and based on one's qualifications, I don't understand how this is possible. How can our health service provide the optimal care if the best men and women for the job are left out in the cold? Why should consultants be given the sole power to make these hiring decisions when it is the HSE and the hospital that is actually hiring the doctors?

What is needed is a properly standardised system to hire all doctors throughout Ireland, involving a single application that is marked independently at the same time each year. The interviews should also be conducted on a single day by a random pool of consultants and HSE staff, based at various centres throughout the country. Consultants should not be allowed to interview candidates for a particular job, but rather should conduct general interviews for the entire country. That way, candidates could be matched to hospitals according to their rating and their order of preference. It is a simple thing to fix, once the will to change is there.

Chapter 11

The Bedlam of Bureaucracy

Proper documentation and consistent organisation are key factors in running a productive, efficient service. Medical documentation is vital: a doctor's notes contain a list of all treatments, illnesses and medications. Without this information, it's impossible for best medical practice to be carried out. Unfortunately, the non-computerised, utterly antiquated system of documentation that props up the Irish health service allows for every kind of confusion, error and time-wasting, not to mention, as I have witnessed, more deadly results.

One such incident involved a mentally ill patient who was admitted to a psychiatric hospital. She was complaining of certain symptoms that did not seem very serious at the time of admission. Nonetheless, she was admitted for observation. A few days' later she appeared to have recovered sufficiently to be discharged, and was sent home. Shortly afterwards, she committed suicide. Given that she was deemed well enough to go home only a short time previously, how did such a gross error of judgment occur?

In this case, the answer was poor documentation. The patient's several years' long history of depression and mental illness had not been taken into account. She had been seen by the team in clinic on one previous occasion, but it had been several weeks since that visit, so they would not have recalled it without the appropriate documentation. On that earlier visit they had been concerned about her welfare, but she had refused admission to the hospital and was not sick enough to be admitted against her will. Her GP had been informed, and it was he who had sent her to the hospital when her condition worsened.

Neither the admitting doctor nor her team at the hospital had access to her notes from the clinic, where she had been treated for the past few years. One glance at those clinic notes would have been enough to jog their memories and ring the alarm bells. Had they had that complete picture of her past history, there is no doubt their assessment would have been different and she would not have been discharged, because she had been assessed as being at risk of suicide just weeks earlier. On this occasion, however, she presented with completely different symptoms and, without the past history to put them into context, the right judgment could not be made. Although most people in the team believed that the outcome would have been different with proper documentation, in the subsequent review by the bureaucratic management there was no acknowledgment that this lack of information had had any role to play.

NOTES AND SCRIBBLES

Each patient has a chart, within which is the sum total of their medical history. Results of scans, x-rays, blood results and operation notes can be found here, as well as a list of their medications to date. The chart is an invaluable tool. When a chart goes missing, calamity ensues because it's simply impossible to treat a patient efficiently without a clear knowledge of his/her past history. A patient is often able to convey this information to the doctor. But quite often time has blurred the clarity of detail. Besides, a patient can't be expected to remember all the finer details and medical jargon of their medical history.

In spite of the importance of charts, they go missing very often. It may be in transit between two departments, or sent down to the typist for dictations, or to the radiologist, or in a pile somewhere on the floor, under a desk, or, on rare occasions, inside the lockers of busy doctors who meant to do something with it but forgot. Each day medical teams waste valuable time looking for charts, old notes and old scans. This is compounded when a patient is new to the hospital and has had some or most of their treatment elsewhere. When this is the case, treatment and investigations have to be put on hold while the necessary documentation is obtained from the other hospitals. This is a difficult and laborious process. First, the new medical team must obtain written consent from the patient to request the information. Then they have to find out which consultant the patient was previously under and pin down the exact days from which they need information. Once this has been sorted, contact is established with the medical records department of the hospital concerned and fax numbers are exchanged. The written consent is faxed to the relevant department, where someone must go and physically search for the file in their archives. When the correct file has been located, the searcher finds the requested pages, photocopies them and faxes them back.

This cumbersome process can take days, during which time the patient's treatment is neither ideal nor efficient. If an administrative error occurs any-where along the chain, the entire procedure begins again from scratch. And all this in an age of advanced technology, when no business would dream of keeping records in a filing cabinet with no back-up system. This is the system the HSE gives hospitals and then expects efficient management of the vast mountain of records accumulated by all medical institutions. No wonder the sentences uttered most often in Irish hospitals today are: 'We can't find the old notes', 'We've requested the old notes but they haven't come up yet', 'We are waiting for the notes to be faxed over.'

That is in the case of single-set notes. It gets even worse when patients have multiple sets of notes from various hospitals. A psychiatric patient who, for example, attends the clinic every few months for check-ups but is also attending a day centre may have changes made to medication and management by the clinic doctor. But there is no guarantee that these will be communicated to the day centre. Why? Because the records showing that the patient attends another service are not adequate. There-fore, the day centre is still dispensing the old pres-cription, in contradiction of what the GP is prescribing based on the clinic appointment.

When the day centre finally gets wind of thi someone has to request faxes from GPs of up prescriptions, then get a doctor to come down and record the prescription at the day centre before the change made at clinic can begin to take effect. A simple administrative issue gets snarled up in gross inefficiency, resulting in delayed and compromised management of patients.

Another typical scenario involves the admission to hospital of acute clinic patients, who may have been well for a considerable period of time but have an extensive known history. A sudden deterioration requires hospitalisation. The doctor assessing, examining and admitting the patient has no access to the notes from the clinic, so the patient history, with its store of valuable information, is lost. The clinic notes are locked away in a building that is not accessible at 4.00am.

The reverse applies, too. A patient who has been admitted acutely to a hospital and then discharged is bought back for review to the clinic a few weeks later. This time it is the doctor at the clinic who is clueless. The patient has been acutely ill and has received intensive management and treatment. He/ t a critical phase of treatment, being ack into the community. There discharge summary, highlighting es of the admission. A copy of this e clinic notes. Usually this copy is by the time the patient is seen at clinic. The system is simply too slow and without the appropriate checks to ensure that the information is passed over in good time. No one is directly responsible for ensuring that this transfer of information occurs. This situation leads to a significantly reduced standard of medical practice, one that is highly inconsistent and involves a great degree of guesswork on the part of the physician. I doubt patients would feel reassured to know that their recovery and continued well-being was reliant on guesswork.

When the notes do finally arrive, they often consist of letters, clinical notes and prescription lists stuffed randomly into a folder, without any consideration to order, chronology or usefulness. In these instances the doctor is lucky to find the note from the previous visit, much less obtain a clear and detailed history of what has been done for the patient thus far at the clinic. The doctor thus finds it very hard to get a clear picture of the background, diagnoses or treatment that the patient has received, which means the unfortunate patient is bombarded with the same questions at every visit.

I have had several irate patients rightly point out to me that the information I'm asking from them should be in their notes. I can't very well stand up and tell them, 'I'm sorry, but your past clinic notes are utter shit and I can't even make out your date of

birth from them, much less anything more useful.'
My advice to every member of the public is to carry
with them to clinic a list of all medications, with
exact dosages. Then, no matter what the quality of
your previous clinic notes, at least the doctor seeing
you will have this vital information to hand.

There are several ways of making these lists. You
can simply gather up all your medication and write
down on a piece of paper the name of the drug and
how many you take at what time of day. The dosage
is usually printed on the bottle, the strip or
covering. Far simpler, however, is to ask your
pharmacist or GP to provide you with an up-to-
date printout at your next visit.

This is only a short-term, band-aid solution. A
comprehensive re-evaluation of the system needs to
be conducted and recommended changes implemented. It is obvious that every branch of the HSE
needs, as a matter of some urgency, a system of data
storage that will bring medical centres in line with
the electronic age in which we live, and will give us a
proper records-management system that will reduce
doubling of work and time-wasting.

THE OUT-PATIENT DEPARTMENT

Many of you will have experienced first-hand the
results of the under-resourcing of our out-patient
clinics, where patients are forced to wait well

beyond their appointment time. Most doctors have been on the receiving end of abuse from tired and frustrated patients who are sick of waiting around without any information on why the delay has occurred, or what their actual appointment time will be.

Despite the best efforts of those of us running the clinics, the system is overcrowded. Furthermore, facilities at these clinics are often substandard in the extreme. There are not enough doctors, but sometimes there are more doctors than there are rooms available to treat patients. The bureaucratic tangle of the HSE creates a monstrous mess. Excessive and unnecessary paperwork is the order of the day. Policy is dictated not by what is right for patients or for society at large, but by concerns about defence lawsuits. In some respects this works to the advantage of medical professionals, in others it does not. Indeed, more often than not it leads to the formulation of ridiculous policy that offers little benefit and makes even less sense from a practical point of view.

I'll give you an example to illustrate the point. One night I was called to review a patient who had been found lying on the floor beside his bed. I saw the patient, spoke to him and examined him. He had slipped down to the floor, but was unhurt. He had been very drowsy on his medication and that was probably a major contributing factor to the fall. I documented the incident in his medical notes, and recommended that any sedating medication be withheld. There was no injury and beyond observation, nothing further was needed at this point. As I prepared to leave the ward, I was stopped by the nurse in charge, who asked me to fill out some forms in relation to the incident.

The first was an incident form. This gargantuan volume can be found in every ward of every hospital in Ireland. Its purpose is to record any incident that might possibly result in the hospital being sued down the line. The manuscript can then be used to provide a record of the incident, outlining what was done at the time and why.

The second was a 'Notification of injury to patient' form. Sub-headings required me to fill in the type of injury to the patient. There was a third form, too. This was not too dissimilar to the second form, but was meant to be completed by nursing staff. The whole thing seemed ludicrous to me. I had already documented everything that had happened in the medical notes. These three forms amounted to pointless duplication.

'But there has been no injury to the patient,' I protested.

'I understand that, but protocol requires us to

fill out these forms, Doctor,' was the nurse's terse reply.

'But the form is titled "Notice of injury to patient". There has been no injury, so what is the point?'

'I know it seems silly, but they ask us to do it.'

Who is 'they'? It was the nurse who was asking me to do this, not some mythical 'they'. Did she not have the common sense to see what a pointless exercise this was? Apparently not. I gave up and filled out the forms, wasting thirty minutes of my time while other patients with more pressing needs were waiting for me.

The health service managers have devised hundreds of these nonsensical bureaucratic protocols, which are adhered to blindly. Any day now I expect to fill out a form after a patient has sneezed. Or to document clearly in the medical notes that the patient has scratched her nose without permission and that she understands and takes full responsibility for all consequences of her action.

ALLOCATING SPARSE RESOURCES

The bureaucracy within the health service is not limited to minor protocols and the running of clinics. It is rife throughout the system. Again, an example to illustrate.

Recently, the Irish government sanctioned monies for the creation of sixteen new full psychiatric teams. The purpose of this windfall was to help ease the inevitable increase in workload that has accompanied the implementation of the Mental Health Act 2001. There is unlikely to be a further spend of this sort in psychiatry for the next five years at least, therefore it is imperative that the resources are used wisely.

Psychiatry, unlike most medicine, which is hospital-based, is community-based. Each county is divided into sectors and each sector has a medical team attached to it. This team includes a psychiatric consultant, one or two junior doctors, occasionally a senior registrar, one or two community psychiatric nurses, a social worker and an administrator. Each team is responsible for the mental health of all the people living within their sector.

When someone falls ill and needs to be admitted to a mental hospital, they are automatically cared for by their sector team, regardless of who is on-call. This is a very enlightened approach to practising psychiatry and can be highly effective. However, it does lead to a lot of in-fighting and transferring of responsibility: 'This patient is not from my area.' This has now taken on an entirely new meaning in light of the extra resources.

In one area of Ireland, the psychiatric service is roughly divided into sectors of equal population. Each sector has its own team. Although the sectors fall into two different counties, the administrative team running them is a joint team, with final oversight on the entire operation. It includes doctors and management staff from both counties.

When the news came of the addition of two full new teams in that area, there were discussions as to how best to allocate the resources. In the end, both of the teams were assigned to the same county. The average population per sector team in that county is 33,000. The addition of two teams would bring that down to around 25,000 for each sector, in other words, a much better situation.

The problem was that the sector most in need of the extra help was in the other county. This particular sector, let's call it sector A, has a population of 55,000. In this case, why were both teams assigned to the same county? There are several reasons. The first mistake was that the crucial meeting took place when some consultants from the impoverished sector were unable to attend. These consultants had been newly appointed to replace out-going consultants and had yet to take up their posts. They had not had the time to assess the need for their sectors and advocate accordingly.

Not alone does sector A, the loser, have the highest population, it also has the population with the greatest need as it is one of the most impoverished areas in the country. (There is an established correlation between socio-economic status and increased incidence of psychiatric illness.) This is evident in the in-patient status of the base hospital for each sector, with in-patient numbers in sector A far exceeding those of the other sectors combined.

The new consultant taking up the mantle of sector A soon realised that it would not be possible to provide quality medical care for so many people with the resources available to him, especially as the population of the sector was set to increase dramatically in the coming years. He then raised objections to the plan, and found himself facing a brick wall. He also got a severe dressing-down from those in charge. There wasn't a problem, he was told. He simply needed to shape up and learn to work more efficiently.

The consultant battled away for weeks. He had to get maps from the Ordnance Survey and combine them with the latest figures from the 2006 census. The HSE data gave the population of his sector as 42,000, but it was in fact 55,000. The gap of 13,000 comprised a group of patients he was looking after, but for whom other consultants were getting the credit.

In the tradition of a health service slow to admit mistakes, the denials continued. They insisted that he had miscalculated, that the original figures were correct. The consultant refused to back down and kept chipping away, writing letters and organising meetings. If one presentation medium failed, he tried another. Eventually, the HSE had to recognise the irrefutable facts: he did have the highest and most needy population, the current level of care for which was bordering on unsafe.

It was with great reluctance that it was finally agreed that it was necessary to re-zone the sectors in sector A's county. A new team would be created, minus any of the additional resources. It would have to come from what was already available in the county. The locum consultant, who had thus far been assigned to cover consultants who were away, would head up the new team. No moves would be made to replace him as locum.

The joint management team of the area understood and recognised the problem, but were apparently powerless to help. The two new teams had been allocated already. This allocation was still purely theoretical, however; no one had even been interviewed for the job. All that was needed was the will to implement change, but, sadly, this was lacking.

For the patients of sector A, the situation will not improve. The number of doctors looking after them will not increase, they will simply be moved around so that there is more superficial parity.

Ultimately, such cosmetic changes will not have any lasting impact. The increasing population in the area will nullify the benefits of the changes, and sector A will be back where it started. Despite battling away and making a villain of himself before his colleagues, the sector A consultant was eventually forced to admit what the bleak truth was: the system will remain the same because the will for change is just not there.

The end result of all this? Nothing really changed and the sector is currently being run contrary to established standards of best medical practice. The consultant who worked so tirelessly to create the optimum environment for his colleagues and his patients now finds himself branded a 'troublemaker' – a catch-all epithet that spells trouble for its holder. When it comes to mental healthcare in this country, it remains a lose–lose situation: the doctors and consultants lose the ability to perform the work to the highest standard; the patients lose their right to the best possible level of care.

Chapter 12

Lost in Translation:

The Growing Communication Gap

n order for any hospital to run efficiently, it is essential that doctors and nurses communicate effectively. Unfortunately, all too often the pressures they are under lead to problems between staff members as everyone strives to do their job in less-than-optimum conditions. Workplace relationships are an important issue in the medical profession and need to be recognised as such so that problems arising can be addressed quickly and resolved.

I believe that the way nursing is managed within the Irish health service has led to severe disillusionment within the profession. Seventy per cent of newly trained nurses in Ireland stop working within three years of qualification. This figure speaks volumes about the quality of life for those who choose this career.

The current implementation of the profession of nursing by the HSE does not allow for it to be run with the compassion, efficiency and professionalism required. Much like junior doctors, nurses are being forced to sacrifice their ideals, and it leaves a bad taste in the mouth. The problems within the ranks come from the top down and include: a zealous adherence to protocol; a lack of adequate training; negative attitudes towards patients who are labelled as 'difficult' for one reason or another; poor communication with medical colleagues, leading to recurrent miscommunication and a widening divide between nurses and junior doctors; a lack of a clear and defined role for nurses; and an aggressive union that is clearly out of touch with the realities of the health service.

Some of the problems stem from ill-thought-out and pointless policies that serve only to force inefficiency upon nursing staff and make their jobs more difficult. Nursing is a challenging enough job as it is, without new problems being foisted on its practitioners from within. Unfortunately, conditions within the Irish health service have deteriorated to the point where it is affecting communication between doctors and nurses. Both parties find

Doctor X

themselves in highly stressful situations, where the pressure is constantly on and there is a severe shortage of time. Under these circumstances, basic courtesy takes a back-seat to getting the job done as quickly as possible. An inadequate number of doctors further exacerbates the problem. The fact that junior doctors often have to turn down or delay valid requests from nurses because they simply have too much to do only serves to create more misunderstanding. On the one hand, junior doctors find themselves stretched and needed in several places at once. On the other, nurses are left holding the ball, waiting, and waiting, for something that needs to be addressed now and not later, but is not as urgent as the matter with which the doctor is currently dealing.

There are some areas that repeatedly throw up difficulties between nurses and doctors. Sleeping pills, for example. There are a few notable drawbacks with sleeping pills: they are highly addictive, they do not treat any illness, they just produce an effect, and users build a tolerance to this effect, so they are never a long-term solution. In general, doctors don't like prescribing sleeping pills to patients, especially in hospitals. Patients are admitted to hospital to have things fixed – the last thing they need is to be sent out with another problem, such as an addiction to sleeping pills or sedatives. This is even

223

more so in the case of the mentally ill. A patient coming into a psychiatric hospital with depression does not need an added addiction to sleeping pills on top of that.

In spite of this, night sedation is one of the cardinal sins of the medical profession. Patients who are soundly asleep do not make demands, they do not kick up a fuss and seek 'unnecessary' attention. The more patients who are sleeping peacefully, the easier the ward is to manage. It is no surprise, then, that many night staff are strong advocates of night-time sedation. It allows them more time to do their tasks properly and follow correct procedures.

There are cases where sleeping pills can be justifiably prescribed, but these are few and far between. For example, in the case of a patient suffering from acute anxiety, it makes sense to use a short-term course of such medication while the cause of the problem is treated. But these are the exceptions, not the rule. Yet to look at patients' charts, you might be led to believe it is the other way round. This 'prescribing for convenience' is harming patients, and it also has an adverse effect on the doctor–nurse relationship because junior doctors are being put under huge pressure to supply these prescriptions. I know for a fact that such medication is often offered to patients on the late night round, then relayed to the doctor on-call as a patient's request. Should the doctor refuse to prescribe it, he may find himself being called down repeatedly by nursing staff on one pretext or another, until he finally gives in. There is a conflict of interest as well as abuse of power at play here.

What we sometimes forget in the medical profession is that the object is not making our jobs as easy as possible, but serving the patient as best we can. Yes, sedation makes for less demanding and irritable patients, but people have a right to be irritable! It is certainly not reason enough to sedate them.

On one occasion during my internship, I refused to prescribe a night sedation. The patient was old and confused, and night sedation would only have increased the risk of him suffering a fall. I convinced the nurse that it was a bad idea. She accepted this explanation, then told me of another intern a couple of years previously who always refused to chart night sedation, no matter what the circumstances. He had argued that it was unsafe to give night sedation to the elderly and that the young could cope without it. This made her job a lot harder, she explained, so she decided to make his life harder in exchange. In the middle of night she would go to patients and pull out IV cannulas that were in perfect working order, so that the doctor in question would be forced to come down and put them back in. I couldn't believe what I was hearing. I was on high alert after that, and thoughts of dirty play occurred whenever a cannula I'd inserted earlier in the day suddenly became dislodged.

Even though that was a single incident with a single nurse, it is incidents like these that create an atmosphere of distrust, in which junior doctors worry that nurses will abuse their power and therefore nurses' requests are treated with suspicion, usually unfairly. The greatest irony here is that neither the nurse nor the doctor is at fault. If we had a shift system, there would be no need for doctors to sleep over in the hospital at night, therefore they wouldn't be called for every problem, big and small, and for every reason, minor and major. When the doctor has been working non-stop for thirty-two to thirty-six hours with very little rest, the line between what is an acceptable reason and an unacceptable reason is drawn very thinly indeed, and differences between how nurses and junior doctors view the issue can escalate quickly, even when both are correct in their point of view.

There is another important factor in relation to sedation that is often overlooked, and it applies to all forms of sedation. Agitation and aggression can often be a sign of deeper illness. This is especially the case in elderly patients. An agitated state may often be the only indication that the patient has suffered a stroke, for example. However, if a patient is sedated as a means of 'treating' the agitation, it could easily mask the symptoms of an underlying problem.

In this context the use of sedation is down right dangerous. You may mask a life-threatening condition, until it's too late. The risk is greatest in patients who are on regular sedatives. They could suffer a 'silent stroke' and nobody around would be any the wiser. That is why I would be a strong advocate against the use of sedative medications in elderly patients. The only exception to this should be when they are acutely unwell and in danger of hurting themselves, or others. But even then the medication would need to reviewed on a frequent basis to justify its continued use.

A root cause of dilemmas such as this, for both doctors and nurses, is the lack of a clearly defined role. Legally, doctors are ranked above nurses in terms of the decision-making process. They are the ones who ultimately must bear the responsibility for any consequences. But nurses will often have invaluable advice and information. The problem is definitely two-sided: where does advice end and interference and pressurising begin? Nurses can feel (rightly or wrongly) that they are not being listened to, while junior doctors can feel (rightly or wrongly) that they are being preached to. This widens the gap, creates distrust and makes the doctor more reluctant to seek advice. The valuable information that experienced nurses can share can thereby get lost, to the detriment of patients and nurse–doctor relationships.

A clear definition of roles would greatly assist in breaking down these artificial barriers and ensuring the smooth operation of each ward. I am very much in favour of nurses prescribing medication, but only if it is done properly. Nurses with experience should be given the necessary training and be allowed to prescribe at least some of the basic medications (especially for drugs that are available over-the-counter outside hospitals). However, with prescribing must come the associated responsibility. While I fully support the efforts of Minister for Health Mary Harney to bring about these changes, it is important that they be implemented with due consideration for the doctor–nurse relationship and with a clear definition of roles in order to avoid lapses in communication.

On the issue of the pressure that is brought to bear on junior doctors to prescribe night sedation, consultants need to take a proactive role. I know of one who was adamant that his patients were never to receive night sedation. If it happened, the next day he would take up the issue with anyone who had so prescribed. The result of this policy was that doctors on-call under this consultant were never pressured by nurses into prescribing sedation inappropriately. When reviewing medications, consultants need to take a strong role in addressing this and making it clear that inappropriate sedation will not be tolerated.

MISUSE OF RESOURCES

Misuse of resources is a significant cause of inefficiency within the HSE. For instance, nurses in many countries, including India and the USA, perform some of the more routine procedures, such as taking blood or inserting IV cannulas. There are many nurses from overseas working in Ireland who are prevented from using certain skills which, arguably, would free up doctors from routine tasks and increase their time for patient care. Yet these nurses often experience pressure from their own colleagues not to carry out these tasks. Why? Because it sets a dangerous precedent. If it were to become the norm, other nurses would be expected to pick up the skill, which would mean more work.

The nursing union must take some of the blame for the current state of nursing because it has been over-zealous in its regulation. A policy of over-protection and over-action has instilled deep-seated inefficiencies in Irish nursing, and these must be addressed. The strike before the general election in 2007 is a clear example of how the union is out of touch with reality. Nurses work a thirty-nine-hour week, which is by no means Draconian. Their starting pay correlates with that of most other health professionals with similar levels of experience, including junior doctors. While I agree that there is scope for an increase in their pay, this is already being addressed by the benchmarking process, which provides the correct arena in which to air any grievances. The strike was wholly unjustified in my view and was not successful either. The union was perceived as being overly aggressive in its tactics, as attacking the ordinary people rather than the politicians. The fact that it was used as a high-profile tactic highlights the disparity between those who represent the nursing profession and the realities of life in modern-day Ireland.

BULLYING

'There is an ingrained culture of bullying in the service. It's how things are done. People are forced to do things they shouldn't be doing.'

This statement was delivered to me by a consultant during a discussion of the issue of bullying and the prescription of inappropriate medications to patients on-call. He agreed there was a high level of tolerance for oppressive attitudes within the health service. He felt these attitudes were not confined to a single group, but rather were endemic throughout: from management, to consultants, to senior doctors, nurses and even junior doctors. The lack of resources has placed everyone under the kind of strain that weakens co-operation and fosters a hierarchy-based governance. The only way to get things done in these unwholesome conditions is by becoming unpleasant. It's a cynical motto: if you don't shaft people, someone else will shaft you.

In an article published in the *British Medical Journal* in 1995, Dr R Lyons described bullying as 'persistent, offensive, abusive, intimidating, malicious or insulting behaviour, abuse of power or unfair penal sanctions which make the recipient feel upset, threatened, humiliated or vulnerable which undermines their self-confidence and which may cause them to suffer stress.'

In October 2005 a study published in the *Irish Medical Journal* arrived at some shocking conclusions: 30 per cent of junior doctors in the south and west of Ireland had been subjected to one or more forms of bullying behaviour, with doctors from non-EU countries reporting much higher rates of bullying than EU doctors. Both groups clearly identified seniors and nursing staff as being the commonest proponents of bullying behaviour.

I have already alluded to some of the bullying of

junior doctors that takes place. This is particularly bad on-call. Little thought is given to the fact that the junior doctor is on a twenty-four to thirty-six-hour shift, as compared to the nurses' twelve- to thirteen-hour shift. Some nurses are, of course, very considerate of this and will keep a list of tasks that need to be done, so that when the doctor has a chance to come down to the ward, they can efficiently finish all the jobs in one go rather than having to run back and forth. But this not always the case: there can be nonchalance and utter lack of consideration, too, making for repeated trips back and forth to the ward, often from far corners of the hospital, for minor problems. This sort of system fosters gross inefficiency and mismanagement of time.

TELEPHONE ORDERS

One policy that is always being hotly debated is that of prescribing-by-phone. As a rule, nurses are not allowed to accept any prescriptions over the phone. It's too risky and they need written proof before they will administer the medication. In many ways this is a sensible policy, but there are instances where it is followed too rigorously.

The most common disagreement occurs at night, and usually with the intern or SHO on-call, who gets a bleep saying that the patient has a headache or other minor ailment and needs some paracet-

amol. It's usually 4.00am and the doctor has just
gone to bed to try and catnap for three hours before
starting the next day. The doctor says yes, it's okay
to give the paracetamol, but is it okay if they come
and chart it first thing in the morning?

Here is where division occurs. Some nurses will
allow for this and take on the responsibility, others
will not and will insist on the doctor coming down
to prescribe it in writing. At first glance the second
option would seem to be the most prudent. However,
the issues surrounding this are more complex and
there is a need to reconsider some aspects of this
rule.

First, we are talking about paracetamol. This is
an over-the-counter medication. It is a very safe
medication, generally speaking. You can give an
adult 4 grams of this over a twenty-four-hour
period without any risk. But it can be dangerous if
too high a dosage is taken, and must also be used
with caution by patients suffering from abnormal
or reduced liver function.

This raises two key points. The first is that you
don't need to be a doctor to prescribe paracetamol,
but it must be taken into account in a hospital
situation that some patients cannot be so prescribed. The second issue is the question of verbal
orders over the phone. If someone rings up claiming
to be a doctor and asks for a medicine to be

prescribed, it could be anyone. In that context it makes sense to not accept telephone prescribing. However, we aren't talking about a random person phoning from God knows where. What we are talking about is a doctor who is replying to a bleep from the ward. When the nurse looks at her phone, the words 'doctors' residence' are flashing, confirming the location of the caller.

It boils down to trust and responsibility. It would be rare that a doctor would make a request like that and not fulfil his side of the deal. I suppose it's easier to stick to protocol and insist the doctor come down, no matter how trivial the issue. But this approach can often cause patients to suffer. What if the doctor on-call is busy dealing with a major emergency and cannot leave his post? Is it fair to make the patient needing paracetamol wait in pain for the doctor to be free?

In the past there has certainly been an unacceptable culture of doctors displaying a disparaging attitude towards nurses. But I believe that has largely changed now and, in fact, in the case of junior doctors, it is often reversed. It is important that doctors and nurses cultivate healthy and friendly working relationships that are complementary rather than antagonistic. It's in the best interests of patients that all their carers are singing from the same hymn sheet.

Chapter 13

Solutions

Arguments, examples and stories mean nothing without concrete proposals to solve the problems inherent in our health system. So here is my checklist of what can be done to create a twenty-first-century health service in Ireland.

1. Dismantle the two-tier system

There is no other way. By definition, the two-tier system creates division: one system for those who can pay extra; another system for those who can't afford the extras. We need one, unified health system with the single goal of providing speedy, efficient, best practice. We need to remove the incentive for consultants to ignore their public duties. We cannot decrease waiting lists until this is done. Our resources should be spent on improving the public health service, not building more private beds so that the wealthy minority can profit from them.

2. More accountability for consultants

As the case of Dr Micheal Neary illustrates so tragically, consultants are really only accountable to themselves, until, that is, it is too late. There should exist regular, independent audits of consultant practice to ensure that mistakes do not get brushed under the carpet or ignored.

Other key areas for change are:

3. A greater contractual responsibility to public healthcare for consultants, to include a minimum number of forty hours per week.

4. The proper availability of twenty-four-hour consultant care.

5. Financial and practical consequences for consultants who neglect their public duties in favour of private practice.

6. Around-the-clock Radiology service that is patient-centred.

7. Outsourcing of Radiology to other countries to meet our growing needs.

8. A standardised protocol for Radiology departments throughout Ireland to ensure a high standard of care.

9. A countrywide increase in the standards of hospital hygiene, along with rewards for meeting them and consequences for hospitals that do not. This will involve performing audits as they ought to be performed: without prior warning.

10. The provision of essential services and materials fundamental to the maintenance of good hygiene.

11. Adequate education and time allocated to the practice of hygienic medicine.

12. A comprehensive twenty-four-hour health service, to include social services, psychiatry and general medical health.

13. Immediate implementation of the European Working Time Directive for doctors, plus a working week for doctors not exceeding fifty hours.

14. A shift system with twenty-four-hour consultant and doctor cover.

15. Fair and equitable procedures for allocating jobs and dismantling of the 'old boys' club' model.

16. A far more focused education about mental health and mental illness to help reduce stigma. The HSE needs to mount an aggressive information campaign to educate the general public as well as its own practitioners.

17. Minimum compulsory mental health training for all doctors and nurses of no less than three to four months.

18. A fair and equitable allocation of resources in all sectors of medicine.

19. A ban on prescription of Xanax and curtailment on prescription of all benzodiazepines.

20. Restoration of dignity, autonomy and respect to the mentally ill.

21. A fair and standardised application process for all medical jobs.

22. A fair and standardised process of promotion and career advancement for doctors.

23. Implementation of electronic storage of patient medical data, with intranet access to health institutions throughout the country.

24. Improved communication between hospitals and health service departments, with emphasis on co-operation rather than competition.

25. Radical increase in the availability of nursing homes and care institutions for the elderly, freeing up much-needed and misplaced acute hospital beds.

26. A sensible review of hospital and nursing protocols.

27. Encouragement of critique and discussion of problems within the system.

28. Eradication of the culture of fear, bullying and intimidation that presently persists, with adequate protection for 'whistleblowers'.

29. Lastly, and arguably most importantly, a dismantling of the power of those with vested interests in the private health service. Those who

stand to gain from the continued poverty of the public health service should not be given a say in how it is run. Be it consultants, managers, government officials or private individuals, if they benefit directly or indirectly from the two-tier health system, then they have a big incentive to maintain the status quo. As long as they hold sway, things cannot improve.

The good news is that the situation isn't past saving and that we can do something about it. But we need to act quickly and decisively. At the present time, health is at the forefront of public consciousness as never before, but for all the wrong reasons. This increasing awareness needs to be turned into a force for positive change. I would encourage everyone out there who has a bone to pick with our health service go make your voice heard. Write to newspapers and contact radio and television talk shows. Lobby your local TD. Question medical professionals, and don't dutifully accept everything they tell you if it goes against your instinct. Forget the 'doctor knows best' dictum your parents taught you. We each have responsibility towards ourselves, and towards one another, to forge the best society we can, and health should be top of our collective to-do list.

Appendix

On RTE's 'Liveline' programme, on 9 January 2007, a young woman, Susie Long, spoke about her diagnosis of terminal bowel cancer – and the delay she has experienced in getting the proper treatment. Her words gave rise to an enormous response, with patients and their families across Ireland sharing both their outrage at her story, and their own bad experiences. On the pages that follow is her heartbreaking letter to Liveline's Joe Duffy, which makes the most eloquent and imploring case imaginable for a fair and equitable healthcare system that treats all patients on the basis of need.

"I'M GOING TO DIE BECAUSE OF HOSPITAL WAITING LISTS"

Dear Joe,

Today I had my 12th session of chemo. I got to talking to the partner of a man who was also getting chemo. She told me that when her partner's GP requested a colonoscopy for him he was put on the waiting list. She then phoned the hospital and told them he had private health insurance and he was seen three days later. He had bowel cancer that was advanced, but had not broken through the bowel wall and spread to other organs. She said the tumour was the size of a fist and what made him go to the doctor (apart from her nagging) was he started to lose weight rapidly. Thank goodness they got it in time and he's going to recover.

I then came home, flicked on the tv and got into bed. The first ad on the tv was from the government telling people that bowel cancer can kill, but not if caught in time. If Bertie Ahern or Mary Harney or Michael McDowell were within reach I would have killed them. Literally. I'm not joking.

Appendix

I don't have private health insurance. It's a long story, so I'll start at the beginning.

I've suffered from digestive complaints for years. It started out with being unable to eat in the mornings or when my stomach felt tense. I'd feel too queasy. Then I got heartburn after just about everything I ate. I lived on Rennies. Then, in 2005, I got a lot of diarrhoea and after a few months it became constant and blood accompanied some of my bowel movements. I went to my GP clinic in the Summer of 2005. Probably about 2 months after the blood started appearing. I look back now and feel stupid for delaying for 2 months, but I wasn't sure if the blood was caused by piles, which my late mother suffered from. I was 39 years old and had read in books and heard a doctor say on tv that bowel cancer doesn't affect people under 50. Anyway, my normal GP was on holiday, but I saw his colleague, and she immediately sent a letter to the local hospital requesting a sonogram and a colonoscopy. Within weeks I was called for a sonogram and was diagnosed with a gallstones. That explained the queasiness and the heartburn. I expected to soon be called for the colonoscopy. I waited through the autumn, then through the start of winter. No word on the colonoscopy and no word on when my gall bladder would be removed.

In November I started to get serious lower abdominal pain after eating. I phoned the consultants secretary and asked if I was on the waiting list. She assured me I was and would be called soon. In December I started to rapidly lose weight. This definitely wasn't like me! I love my food, Joe. I phoned the hospital again after Christmas. Again I was told that I was still on the list and would definitely be called soon. (I later found out that that consultant had retired and they had just hired a new one). Joe, from November to the end of February I was in agony. Apart from the pain and diarrhoea I was tired all the time. I'd literally got out of bed to go to work at 4.30 in the afternoon. Came home around 10.30pm, ate my dinner (I couldn't eat before work because it'd make me too sick to do my job), tidied the kitchen and went to bed again. I was miserable.

Finally, on February 28, 2006, four days after I turned 40, I was called for a colonoscopy.

I woke up in the middle of the procedure and saw on a large screen, them probing a blob on my colon. They were taking a biopsy. But I didn't have to wait for the results. I knew what I had. Soon after I met my wonderful consultant, Dr George Nassim. What a gem he is. Friendly, compassionate and funny on top of being a great surgeon. I felt like I was in good hands. I didn't panic for more than a few hours after I was told that I had cancer. They can do loads of things to save cancer patients these days. I was young and strong. I'd been a vegetarian since I was 16. I ate mostly healthy foods, although eating at night was a serious no-no when it came to my weight. I went for walks a few times a week. I felt I could beat this.

I was booked in for surgery to remove the tumour. I was given a stoma, which means I'll have to poop in a bag for the rest of my life. I found that really difficult to handle. More difficult than the cancer sometimes. I was in St Luke's hospital for over 50 days last year. (I had to have a second surgery due to complications) Recovery was hard, but I did it. I shared a room with two lovely women who also had cancer. They have since died. In another ward I was in I was next to another woman who had cancer. She died too. The staff at St Luke's in Kilkenny are the most kind, hardworking people I've ever met. In March, in between surgeries, I was sent to the Mater in Dublin and had a porto-cath put in for putting the chemo through, and a PET Scan to see if the cancer had spread. If it hadn't, I'd live. If it had spread to other organs, I'd die. It had spread to my lungs.

I felt bad enough to go to the doctor. She did what she was supposed to do. She told them I had diarrhoea and blood from my rectum. But what could they do? So do lots of people. Should I have skipped the list ahead of those other people with the same symptoms? I don't think so. Should there be a list so long that it puts people at risk of dying? No. Definitely not.

I know in my heart and soul that when I started to feel really, really bad, especially in from December to February 2006, is when the cancer broke through the wall of my bowel. Of course I can't prove it. But I know. Because it broke through the bowel I have been given 2 to 4 years from diagnosis to live. The chemo is to prolong life, not to save it. I have 3 years, tops, to go. Despite that, I'm going to try my best to make it for 5 more till my youngest turns 18. He needs me too much now. My husband has suffered right along side of me in his own way knowing that the woman he loves will be dead soon. My 18-year-old daughter has been told and has gone quiet and doesn't want to talk about it. But I know she's scared. I haven't told my 13-year-old son yet. He's too young to handle it. The South East Cancer Foundation in Waterford have been very helpful and will help us when the time is right to do and say the "right" things.

I don't blame the wonderful people who work in St Luke's in Kilkenny. They work with what they are given. St. Luke's has the best A&E unit in the country. I had to use it three times in 2006 and twice with my son (nothing serious, thankfully). What did the government do? Threaten to shut it down. They also threatened to shut down the maternity unit AFTER spending millions to improve it!! That would mean Carlow women would have to travel to already overcrowded hospitals in Dublin and Kilkenny women would have to travel to Waterford, which is grand if you live in South Kilkenny. The rest could lump it and birth at the side of the road if necessary.

Twice I had to listen to two women die next to me in hospital because there's no place for people nearing death and their loved ones to go to die and grieve in dignity.

My time in the Mater was dreadful. I was terrified I'd pick up MRSA because it was filthy. I was put on a ward with cardiac patients, mostly men, who because of their ill health were unable aim too well when they went to the toilet. Once when I used the toilet my pajama bottoms soaked up urine up to my ankles. Even though I was still sick and weak I still tried to hover over the toilet so I wouldn't have to touch it. I wasn't able to hover and hold up my pajama legs at the same time. I had just given my sister-in-law two sets of pj's to take home and wash and had nothing to change into. I rinsed them out in the grimy sink and wore them damp until she returned the next day with clean ones. There was excrement stuck to the sides of the toilet for days at a time. Water flooded the shower room, soaked my clean pjs and towel that were on the floor outside the shower and ran out into the hall. After that happened the first time I learned to take a chair in to the shower room to put my stuff on. At least I knew THAT floor got water and soap put on it regularly. The man in the bed next to me, who had suffered a triple bi-pass was served up a greasy fry for tea when he had specifically ordered fish because it was healthier. On the third day he refused to eat it when they wouldn't give him what he had ordered and went without eating on principle. I was vegetarian and so was served cheese on crackers and cheese sandwiches (fake cheese slices on white bread) for all but two meals. They brought one of the two nicer meals when I was fasting and not allowed to eat it. My suspicion is that the catering has been privatised, although I could be wrong. The staff, apart from one really nasty nurse, were lovely.

Should I blame anyone for my hard luck? I've thought about it over the last year and have tried to be reasonable about it. After all, I waited to get Christmas over with before I phoned the hospital for a second time asking to be seen. But today, when I heard that a very nice man who was in the same, if not worse condition, than me when he went to his GP is going to live because he had private health insurance and I'm going to die because I didn't, I had to bite my tongue. I'm happy he's going to live. He deserves to live. But so do I. Then I came home and watched that ad which told people to hurry up and get checked out for bowel cancer because it will save their lives, and I fucking lost it.

I've finally reached the angry stage, I guess. Who am I angry at? I'll tell you, Joe. The health service has been in the hands of Fianna Fail and the PD's for years and all they can think to do is put resources into privatisation. They don't have the ability to change structures in the public sector that would put more resources toward patient care. But it's not just the politicians. I'm also angry at every single voter who voted for Fianna Fail and the PDs because they thought they'd get a few more shillings in their pockets but were too greedy and stupid to realise that that money they saved in wage taxes would be made up with stealth taxes. We all knew before the last election what their health policies were and the majority of people ignored this and voted for them anyway. Maybe they thought this would never happen to them. Or maybe because so many have private health insurance they just didn't care because they were alright, Jack.

I never dreamed I'd get cancer, let alone die from it. But I was wrong. My message to anyone with symptoms of bowel cancer is go to your GP immediately. If you, like me, don't have health insurance, pester them until they hate you, go to your politicians and beg them to help, go to the media, get a solicitor to threaten to sue the government and the hospital if they don't get you in soon for a colonoscopy. Otherwise, the people who love you might lose you and you'll not get to do all the things you planned in life.

I'm writing to you because the way this country is run leads me to believe that contacting a radio show is the only way to try to change things like this. I hope that when Ms SUV and Mr Builder goes into the voting booth, they'll think about me, my husband and especially my children. My husband is a decent man. He works full time in a good job and I worked part-time in a job I loved that helped people, but didn't pay well. It depended on government money to help women and children in crisis, so of course couldn't pay me well. We know what Bertie, Michael, Micheal and Mary's priorities are.

Despite one and a half incomes we couldn't afford VHI or Bupa. But even if we could have we wouldn't have gotten it because we believed (and still do) that all people should get good care despite their incomes. We thought jumping queues was wrong. We're socialists . . . just like Bertie. Ha Ha. Now I feel like vomiting and it's not the chemo!

From a cancer patient in Kilkenny

Author's Acknowledgements

Writing this book has been a rewarding but difficult process, one that would not have been possible without the help of certain individuals. For their invaluable help, support and time, I would like to thank my agent, Faith O'Grady of the Lisa Richards Literary agency, for championing the project and helping the manuscript find its way to the right hands; my editor, Ciara Considine at Hodder Headline Ireland, for her endless patience, wisdom and hard work; medical colleagues and consultants who provided encouragement, and moral and practical support from the start; GC, a great friend and an honest man; and last, but not least, my spouse, who reassured and advised me in my moments of greatest doubt.